90p

THE
Busy Mother's
COOK BOOK

THE
Busy Mother's
COOK BOOK

Patsy Kumm

FABER AND FABER
3 Queen Square
London

First published in 1972
by Faber and Faber Limited
3 Queen Square London WC1
Printed in Great Britain by
Western Printing Services Ltd, Bristol
All rights reserved

ISBN 0 571 09899 1

Acknowledgements

To my husband and children who acted as willing – and highly critical – guinea-pigs. To the many friends and relations who've let me plunder their own recipe store for this book. And to Cannon Industries, who rushed me a cooker to use for testing purposes when my own gave up the ghost.

Contents

CONTENTS

CHAPTER ONE

An Introduction

▨▨

Why *another* cookery book, to add to the hundreds published every year? The answer's a selfish one.

Over the years, I've hunted for a book like this, and not found it. I've discovered cookery books on preparing quick meals that seem to assume either that you want to live on eggs or salads, or that you'll manage on nothing but tins, packets, and speedy expensive things like steak and fresh salmon. I've read books on feeding children that are packed with good, sound traditional recipes and ways of making rice pudding temptingly rainbow coloured, or concocting Hansel and Gretel cottages out of sponge cakes. Which wasn't what I needed to know at all.

Finally, I decided that if I wanted a whole, ready-reference range of budget-conscious recipes, suited for feeding a family of six, and with plenty of fresh produce included – I'd better assemble it myself. Once half-way, it seemed sense to extend the whole idea into a book.

So here it is. And here's something about the recipes you'll find in it, and how to use them.

For a start, though I've included some special occasion recipes the emphasis is on economy. Few mothers feeding a family these days can afford otherwise. Convenience foods play a part, of course, because of their time-saving potential, but this isn't a 'Jiffy-meals-out-of-cans' sort of book. Apart from a few store cupboard suggestions, tinned and packet goods are used to supplement fresh ones, rather than replace them. Or they're used when the fresh versions might be too expensive, or unobtainable.

Unless stated otherwise, all recipes allow for six healthy appetites

– Mum's, Dad's, and four children's. Because even if you don't have four offspring of your own, there's often one with a double-size appetite, or a couple of extra kids sitting down to table.

Where possible, ingredients are given in cup or spoon measures, which saves the need for getting out your scales and having weighing sessions. The spoon and cup measures are the common ones sold in kitchen or hardware departments of good stores. If you don't have – or want to buy – any, borrowing from a friend who does possess them will soon make it clear which of your own cups and spoons are the right size, and you can use those. Otherwise, ordinary cups and spoons are generally good enough, since none of the recipes depend on such hairbreadth accuracy that a little either way will hurt.

Some ingredients, you'll see, are given in pounds or pints, or parts of either, when it seems more logical to measure them that way. For instance, it's simpler to mark off a packet of butter or lard in a 3-ounce slice than to do it by cup or spoon. A pint of milk is easily tipped from the bottle, and meat and vegetables can be bought in the right amount.

When it comes to equipment, I'm not assuming that you've got an electric mixer, liquidiser, pressure cooker, or any other expensive gadget. (If you do have super automated aids you'll know how and when to use them to cut down hard slog, and processes will be quicker still.) Some basic tools are vital, of course, and I've listed them in Chapter Two. I've also given sizes of baking tins used throughout this book, which will stop frustration and time wasting caused by discovering that you don't possess a set of éclair tins, or a flip-sided, loose bottomed cake tin, and what on earth can you use instead? Sorting out situations like this takes time that no busy Mum can afford, and talking of time saving, Chapter Two's got some thoughts on that.

Looking for traditional dishes – Christmas Pudding, Roast Beef with trimmings, Steak and Kidney pie? Don't bother to search here! There are masses of books containing these, all concisely and expertly explained so I don't see any point in repeating them here. Searching for soufflés, syllabubs and puff pastry recipes? Unless you want new, quick variations you won't find these either, because books on entertaining and gracious eating go into the making of these in greater depth than I'd presume to do.

What you *will* find here are foods you can knock up quickly and easily while the children mill ravenously round the kitchen. Foods to pre-cook or prepare a day or more in advance, in anticipation of looming, hectic times. Plus bulk prepared mixes to store and draw on when needed.

And for anyone who feels concerned, from time to time, about whether or not they're feeding their children healthily, Chapter Three takes a special look at this very point.

In short – I hope that the ideas here will be ones you'll find useful and enjoyable. That you'll want to take many of them up because they fit into your busy life as they do into mine, and into the lives of the many friends who've passed their favourite recipes on to me.

CHAPTER TWO

Time and Temper Savers

The less time you have for feeding the family, the more systematic you need to be. Same thing goes if you don't *enjoy* cooking. One of the most efficient cooks I know has become that way because she loathes it so much that she's built up a routine to get her out of the kitchen as fast as possible.

Over the years, most of us establish our own special time and temper savers. But if you have a sneaking suspicion that you could do with refreshing your ideas, this chapter may be helpful.

Begin by bringing office organisation into the kitchen. Put up a notice board, and pin onto it shopping lists, recipes to try out, and special offer coupons to use next time you go out shopping (not to mention pinning the shoe repair and cleaning tickets where you can actually find them!).

Hang constantly-used things like wooden spoons, frying slices, colander, saucepans and so on, near the place they're most often needed – usually the cooker. After all, if it's true that the 'Average Housewife' covers between 5 and 10 miles each day, putting a pressure of about 1,500 tons on her feet, the more than can be done to lighten the load, the better.

Keep small containers of herbs, spices and other flavourings in a cardboard box or on a small tray. This groups them tidily, and prevents the small things sneaking their way behind the large.

Store a tablespoon measure in containers of things you usually measure that way – flour, sugar, bulk mixes and so on. It'll speed up preparation.

Cover shelves with cheap blotting paper that absorbs spills. When it becomes grotty it's quick and easy to replace. Cover floors with sheets of newspaper or plastic when you're having a hefty cooking session, or when the weather's foul and children are bombing in and out. Scraps of peel, dustings of flour and lumps of mud and grass will drop on the paper, so all you do when you're ready to tidy is to gather up the paper and fling everything in the dustbin. Underneath – a clean floor!

Avoid lengthy, depressing cooker cleaning sessions by keeping it spick and span as you go along. Give it a quick one minute wipe over a day, instead of letting grime harden – it's quicker in the long run. Remember that an oven wipes easier while it's still warm. Line the grill pan with foil – and line trays under gas burners the same way (not with electric cookers, though, when it could be dangerous).

Roasting meat in foil or in a lidded dish, for most of the time, will keep your oven cleaner and cut the need for meat basting, too (when cooking in foil, however, allow the same length of time but set the oven slightly higher). For open roasting, bear in mind that if meat is cooked *longer* at *lower* temperature, it will make less mess than if it's roasted for a *shorter* time, spluttering away at a *higher* temperature.

Ovenproof casseroles and baking tins wash more easily if you grease them before use, paying special attention to corners and top edges. Milk pans come clean more speedily if they're rinsed before use with cold water . . . a scrambled egg pan, if you've lightly greased the base before cooking the eggs.

Stocking Up

Biggest time-waster of all is having to keep popping to the shops for this extra ingredient or that, because you can't carry on with the meal preparation unless you do. Bulk buying is one way to reduce the chances of this happening, and it often saves you money too. And theoretically, following the lists just coming up would stop you running low on supplies.

STORE CUPBOARD ITEMS

With the items listed below on your shelves, or in the refrigerator, you'll know that you have *all* the etceteras needed for all the dishes in this book. Plus some ingredients that are in themselves the basis of extra quick meals.

The list may look alarmingly long, but a glance through it is almost bound to show that you have plenty of the items already. (Tick them off if you like – this is a cook book to *use*!) Gradually, you can build up the rest. After which, it's just a matter of keeping a list pinned inside your store cupboard door, or on your notice board, and writing down anything that's used up, so that you remember to buy it next time you go shopping.

Here goes then . . .

Dry Goods

Baking powder

Bicarbonate of soda

Biscuits

  ginger snaps

  savoury crackers, small and large

  wholemeal or sweetmeal

Breadcrumbs (dried, shop-bought or own make)

Cereals

  All Bran

  cornflakes

  Rice Krispies

Citric Acid

Coconut, desiccated

Cornflour

Cream of tartar

Crisps

Custard powder

Dried fruits

  chopped, mixed candied peel

  currants

  dates

  glacé cherries

  mixed dried fruits (apricots, apple, etc.)

  prunes

  raisins

  sultanas

Flours

  plain

  scofa meal

self-raising
wholemeal

Nuts
  almonds – flaked and ground
  chestnuts
  hazelnuts
  peanuts
  walnuts

Oatmeal, medium

Oats, porridge

Pastas
  macaroni
  noodles
  spaghetti

Pulse foods
  butter beans
  haricot beans
  split peas

Rice
  ground and long grain

Semolina

Stuffings, your favourites

Suet, shredded

Sugars
  caster
  demerara
  granulated
  icing
  soft brown

Milks

Canned cream
Evaporated

Instant, non-fat, skim-milk
  powder
Sweet, condensed

Spices, Dried Herbs and Other Seasonings

Anchovy paste

Black pepper

Bouillon cubes, chicken and
  beef

Capers

Caraway seeds

Cayenne pepper

Celery salt

Curry powder

Fruit chutney and sweet pickle

Garlic/garlic powder

Gherkins

Herbs
  basil
  bay leaves

chives

marjoram or oregano

mint

mixed

parsley

rosemary

sage

tarragon (optional)

thyme

Mango chutney

Marmite

Mustard

  English

French

Paprika, sweet

Piccalilli

Salt

Sauces

  1,000 Island Dressing

  Soy

  sweet and sour

  Tabasco

  Worcester

Vinegar (wine, white, malt, tarragon are all mentioned, but you can always substitute one for the other)

Sweet Flavourings and Syrups

Almond essence

Chocolate

  cooking, plain

  sweet (powder and bar)

  vermicelli or chips

Cinnamon

Cloves

Cocoa powder

Coffee

  essence

  instant powder

Ginger, ground

Golden syrup

Mixed spice

Nutmeg

Ovaltine

Rum essence

Treacle

Vanilla essence

Canned or Packet Soups and Sauces

Canned soup

  mulligatawny

  tomato

Condensed soups

  celery

  cream of chicken

mushroom

tomato

Packet sauces

  cheese

  curry

parsley

Packet soups

  minestrone

  mushroom

  onion

Canned Fruits

Apple purée (for when you have none made)

Apricots

Blackcurrants

Cherries, preferably Morello

Grapefruit segments

Peach slices

Pear halves

Pie fillings – apricot, black-currant etc.

Pineapple juice

Pineapple titbits and rings (though rings can be chopped to make titbits)

Raspberries

Convenience Vegetables (canned, frozen, etc.)

Baked beans

Beanshoots

Carrots

Green beans

Peas

Potato powder (instant)

Sweet corn

Tomatoes

Tomato purée

Canned Meats

Chopped ham with pork (approx. 14 oz.)

Corned beef (approx. 12 oz.)

Luncheon meat (approx. 12 oz.)

Chicken curry (recipe requires two large cans)

Fish

Anchovy fillets

Cod fries, frozen (recipe requires two packets)

Pilchards, 1 lb. can

Salmon

Sardines

Shrimps or prawns

Tuna (7 oz. cans)

Extras

Baker's yeast (only needed for
    ginger beer)

Brandy snaps

Brown ale

Caramels

Casilan (only needed for
    Yoghurt)

Chocolate flavour dessert

Chocolate peppermint creams

Cider, dry

Cidrax

Cocktail onions

Corn oil (for baking, cooking)

Dried flakes of apple, celery
    and onion (not essential but
    a useful standby)

Ginger, preserved (optional)

Honey, thin

Jam
    blackcurrant
    raspberry

Juices
    grapefruit
    lemon
    orange
    pineapple
    tomato

Lemon curd

Lemon jelly slices (optional)

Marshmallows

Mayonnaise and/or salad
    cream

Mincemeat

Orange marmalade, thick cut

Orange squash

Peanut butter

Processed cheese spread,
    plain and flavoured

Rice pudding (canned)

Sandwich spread

Sherry

Stuffed olives (optional)

Vanilla ice cream (in freezer)

Store cupboard note: They're not specifically mentioned in recipes, but remember that Long Life milk and cream, packed in foil lined cartons, keep without refrigeration for up to 6 months (for milk) and at least 2 months (for cream). Also, freeze-dried vegetables are more compact to store than cans, and lighter to carry; and don't take up freezer space like frozen vegetables.

FRESH INGREDIENTS

Fresh ingredients can't be kept permanently on hand unless you've got a deep freeze. But when you've had no time to pre-plan, just look at the ingredients below and decide which to buy – knowing you'll find at least two (and probably more) recipes for using them. Then, if your store cupboard's up to date, and if you have a fresh vegetable or two, you don't have to think any more till you get back home again.

I've also listed the 'extra' fresh ingredients, like breads and dairy goods, used in this book.

Meats

Bacon slices
Beef
  joint for roasting
  minced
  stewing
  topside or brisket
Chicken
  joints
  whole
Ham or bacon joint
Ham slices
Lamb
  breast
  chops and cutlets
  joint for roasting
  minced
  stewing

Liver
  lamb's or pig's, though others may be substituted
Pork
  blade bone
  chops
  lean (meat from any good cut)
  streaky (belly)
Salami
Sausages
  chipolatas
  frankfurters
  ordinary large
  small skinless
Veal
  minced
  stewing

Fish

Cod steaks or fillets

Haddock
  fresh
  smoked

Kippers

Mackerel

Sprats

Whitebait

Dairy Goods and Fats

Butter, salted and unsalted

Cheeses
  Cheddar
  Cheshire
  Cottage
  Cream
  Danish Blue
  Lancashire
  Parmesan

Cream
  double (buy or make your
  own, see p. 44)
  whipping

Eggs, large and standard

Lard

Margarine, luxury for quick
  blending and spreading;
  harder for other uses

Milk

Natural yoghurt (bought, or
  home-made – pp. 156, 157)

Shortening (lard, etc.)

Vegetables (actually used in recipes)

Beetroot (optional)

Broad beans

Cabbage, white

Carrots

Celery

Chestnuts

Chicory

Chives

Cucumber

Garlic, fresh

Leeks

Lettuce

Marrow

Mint

Mushrooms

Onions
  ordinary
  shallot

spring	red
Parsley	Potatoes
Peppers	Sweet corn cobs
green	Tomatoes

Fruits

Apples, eating and cooking	Raspberries
Bananas	Rhubarb
Blackberries	Strawberries
Lemons	White grapes, seedless
Oranges	

Breads

| Brown bread | Soft breadcrumbs, fresh |
| Granary or fruit – malt loaf | White bread |

KITCHEN EQUIPMENT

Some equipment's nice to have, but not *necessary* – and I'll come to that in a while. Meanwhile, these are the items that I consider pretty essential. When it comes to baking tins, I've given the sizes used throughout this book; if yours are different, remember that this may affect cooking time and ingredient quantities.

Small sharp knife
Large sharp knife
Set of spoon measures and cup measures (or ordinary spoons and cup for measuring that you know are the right size, see p. 12)
Jug marked in fluid measures (pints, fluid ozs. etc.)
Wooden spoons, different sizes, for stirring
Chopping board
Rolling pin (though an empty milk bottle will do)

Lidded containers for storage of mixes, and of biscuits, cakes etc. These can be plastic or glass, so long as the lids make them airtight

Colander

Grater

Mincer

Kettle

Frying pan

Egg whisk or beater

Frying slice

Sieve (for straining any lumps from gravy, custard etc. – great time saver)

Spatula

Various sizes bowls, jugs etc. for storing and mixing

Set of saucepans, from small to very large

Various shaped and sized ovenproof dishes

Kitchen foil

Greaseproof paper

Brush, for applying glazings to pies etc.

Paper baking cases

Baking tins as follows:

Baking tin 12″ × 9″ × 2¼″ deep (for larger slab cakes and bakes). It could be the Sunday roasting tin, foil lined

Oblong baking tin, 10″ × 6″ × 1¼″ deep

1-lb. and 2-lb. loaf tins for cakes, breads, etc.

Square baking tin, 7¼″ × 7¼″ × 1¼″ deep

Round flan tin, 10″ diameter

Two sponge tins, 7½″ diameter

Cake tins, 8″ and 10″ diameter

Ring tin, 8½″ total diameter, and 2½″ deep, with a 3″ diameter hole in the middle

Large shallow baking tray, 12″ × 9″, for cookies etc.

USEFUL EXTRA EQUIPMENT

Some people are so gadget mad that they compulsively buy more and more. The danger being that, in the end, they have so many that the sheer palaver of deciding which to use causes more bother than brevity, more washing up than speeding up.

However, there are some excellent kitchen aids, and it's sensible to gradually acquire ones which will really step up your pace *or* make jobs you most dislike less tedious.

Here are my suggestions, starting with the smaller things and working up to larger ones which you might consider when you need to replace existing equipment, and when you can afford them:

A 'Mouli' grater, for quick and easy grating of cheese, nuts, etc.

A potato peeler – the sort with a rotating blade. If you have an electric mixer that also takes a potato peeler, this is a terrific asset.

An auto chopper, that cuts up onions, carrots and other raw vegetables as large or small as you want, in seconds.

A rotary egg beater – the better the quality, the smoother the action.

A Tala Cook's Measure, which is printed with names of everyday ingredients (flour, sugar, rice, etc.) and marked out in amounts for each ingredient (4 oz., 6 oz., 8 oz. etc.). It gives useful cup and pint measures, too.

A really plump cook's brush, which makes nifty work of greasing baking tins, and brushing pastry with egg or milk.

An asbestos mat for things you want to simmer as slowly as possible. The less controllable your hot plate temperature, the more important this is.

A wide-mouthed vacuum flask for keeping drinks hot to greet home-coming children on winter evenings; for keeping a meal, or soup, warm when there's a latecomer to a meal (cheaper than leaving on the oven).

Kitchen stationery, like silicone paper, see-through wrapping film, paper towelling and foil pudding basins and dishes. None of these things are cheap, but they can simplify life. Non-stick silicone paper can be used to line baking trays or to wrap up food. Paper towelling deals handily with spills, and spreads on surfaces to keep them clean when you're doing a really messy job. As for foil pudding basins and dishes, they're good for leftovers and for re-heating smaller portions, and though they can be washed, if they're really dirty you just throw them away.

An electric pinger to remind you that a cake needs removing from the oven, or that it's time to put on the vegetables.

A stainless steel 'chipper' if your family are chip addicts.

A pressure cooker. I've had one for seventeen years, and couldn't keep up to schedule without it. It can take not only minutes but literally hours off total cooking time (a stew takes about 20 minutes; cabbage, barely 2 minutes), and it tenderises tougher, cheaper cuts of meat. What's more, home-made soups can become everyday standbys instead of rare treats, lengthily prepared.

An electric mixer, for quicker, simpler baking sessions.

An electric blender, for liquidising cooked vegetables or fruits into purées; or transforming cooked vegetables with stock or water into soup; or blending milk shakes, fruit fools and other desserts.

A cooker with automatic oven. This means you can put an un-cooked meal (or one to be re-heated) into the oven before going out, and come home to find that the oven has switched itself on and cooked the meal. If you're late, the heat will automatically be turned off. It's not something you'd go out and buy on a whim, but it's well worth considering if you need to replace your cooker at any time. Buying a new cooker, too, look for features like simmer control hot plates, see-through glass doors, self-cleaning mechanism or oven lining that comes out for easy cleaning.

A deep freeze. Either to store bulk-bought commercial frozen products; *or* to buy meat and vegetables in bulk at cheap prices, and store them; *or* to freeze garden produce, and cakes, casseroles, sauces, etc. that you make in bulk to cut time and oven-heat costs.

SPEEDING UP FOOD PREPARATION

Remembering that one woman's short cut is another's long haul, here's a miscellany of tips garnered from friends and friends of friends. See which suit you best.

Baking

When you have to roll out any kind of dough (bread, pastry, biscuit), do it between sheets of waxed paper. It breaks and sticks less, doesn't make as much mess, and if you're keeping the rolled dough in one piece, you can use the paper to lift it up to the tin or pie dish.

Breakfast

If early a.m.'s your worst time of day, make a point of assembling breakfast ingredients the night before – removing bacon rinds, pricking sausages, etc. If you plan to have scrambled eggs, beat them and leave them in a cool place in a covered basin; beat again for a few seconds in the morning. Lay the table the night before, too, or get the children to do it. It's one less thing to worry about.

Dairy Products

If *milk* boils over, you're not only wasting it but you'll take precious time mopping it up. So prevent it happening. Either by placing a Solidex disc (or upturned saucer) in the pan, to stop over-boiling. Or by greasing the top rim of the pan so that the milk can't 'climb' easily up the sides.

Remember that *egg whites* whip faster if you add a pinch of salt, but won't whip well if you get a drop of water or speck of yolk in the bowl . . . that both egg whites and *cream* whip more quickly when they're cold.

27

If you go to use *cooking fat*, and find it hard, rub it down a grater first, to save blending time. And if *butter* straight from the refrigerator is hard and will take some time to soften and spread smoothly, add 1 tsp. boiling water to every 2 oz. butter, and beat well before using.

Jellies

To make them set more quickly, use only half the stated amount of boiling water to dissolve jelly cubes, then make the liquid up to its usual quantity by adding ice cubes. Stir in till dissolved before leaving to set.

Leftovers

No busy Mum can afford to despise leftovers, because the fact that they're ready cooked means they cut time corners. So much so, that there are some things which I always cook too much of on purpose. Like *macaroni*, which can be stirred into cheese sauce. Like *rice*, because apart from re-heating it to serve as an accompaniment, it can be mixed with fried onion, meat leftovers, chopped green pepper, and chopped fried bacon, or whatever's around, and made into a savoury pilaf.

If you've some leftover *short pastry*, roll it out as one flat piece, and bake in the oven at the same time as you bake whatever it is you're making. When cooked, break it up with a fork, and mix with either grated cheese and a good pinch of herbs, or with caster sugar and spice. Store, ready to use as topping for a savoury or sweet dish.

Leftover, not-so-fresh *plain cake* is good cut into thickish slices, and fried in butter till crisp. Or crumble it up into crumbs, stir in an extra sprinkling of brown sugar, and use as a crumble topping. Old *fruit cake*? Crumble it up with an egg, and perhaps a dash of milk, to a pudding consistency, then bake in a hot oven for about 20 minutes; serve as a pudding with custard or tinned cream.

Egg yolks, remaining after using the whites, can be covered with cold water and stored in a covered dish in the refrigerator. Here, they'll keep several days (or they can be deep frozen, as can egg whites). Use them to add extra nutriment to mashed potatoes, or stir them into hot soup before serving (don't let soup boil after you add the egg yolks, though). Or use them to glaze the pastry top of a pie, before baking it.

Egg whites can be kept for a few days, too, in a covered container in the refrigerator, and used for making meringues (see p. 219) as and when you have time.

Hard-boiled eggs will stay good for nearly a week in a refrigerator, so long as they're still snug in their shells. They come in handy for sandwiches, spur of the moment egg curry, egg mayonnaise . . . for serving in a salad, or in a cheese sauce on creamed potato.

If *scones* are left from tea-time, cut them in half, moisten the halves with melted butter and brush with beaten egg before sprinkling with caster sugar. Bake in a hottish oven for 14–20 minutes, and they'll taste delicious and fresh. Or use them sprinkled with grated cheese to top a savoury dish – it makes a change from a pastry lid.

When any of the *joint* is left over from your roast dinner, try cutting the meat into paper thin slices, laying the slices on hot plates, then masking them with piping hot gravy or sauce. This will heat the meat, and be kinder to both the taste and texture of the meat than if you re-heated it in the gravy, in the oven.

Finally, do you ever over-estimate the amount of *butter icing* or *butter cream* you make for a cake? Next time, use what's left to sandwich together plain sweet biscuits, and serve them as a tea-time special!

Meat

A *roast joint* in itself is no trouble at all. It's the trims that keep you slogging in the kitchen, and create piles of washing up. So forget tradition. Cook jacket potatoes instead of roast ones – cook carrots with knobs of butter in a covered dish in the oven (see p. 117) or serve the meat with a side plate of green salad tossed in dressing.

If a recipe calls for *slices of meat*, ask the butcher to cut it that way when you buy it – his knives are probably sharper and more practised than yours. Same with *minced meats* of any kind (the Terrine on p. 164 is prepared in a few minutes when the mincing is done for you). Unless you choose a moment when the shop's packed, most butchers are pretty obliging.

Ready-Mixes

Certain things needed often in recipes can be mixed and stored, ready for use. For instance, store a *vanilla pod* in a well lidded jar of caster sugar, and do the same thing with a stick of *cinnamon*. When you make cakes, biscuits or puddings needing these special flavourings, the impregnated sugar does the job.

Have *seasoned flour* ready in a canister, allowing 2 level tsp. salt and 1 of pepper to each ½ lb. flour (or fix your own preference). Alternatively, leave the flour plain but mix up the seasoning – two parts salt to one of pepper – and keep that in a salt cellar.

Learn the value of making up *your own mixes* for cakes, puddings, batters, etc. This gives you all the convenience of the bought packet kind, at far less cost. Page 38 starts off the section in this chapter telling you all about it.

Rice

Remember that rice can be cooked in advance, kept in a refrigerator, and re-heated (more on p. 103).

Stock

You can keep *beef or chicken stock* for up to 7 days in a covered container in the refrigerator. With this on hand, a hearty soup or sauce can be made in a hurry ... or use it instead of water when cooking vegetables, for extra flavour.

Vegetables

Buy them washed when possible. Prepare them, and salad things, for at least two meals at a time. Store *green vegetables*, prepared but unwashed, in a polythene bag in the refrigerator. Prepare *root vegetables* in advance; cover with cold water and put in a cold place

– they do lose a little of their nutritive value, so don't make it a regular habit. *Potatoes* keep for up to a week in cold water in the refrigerator, if you change the water every day.

Potatoes can be pre-cooked, too. Choose large ones, and cook them in their jackets, either steaming them over hot water till tender, or pressure cooking them according to instructions given for the cooker. When they're done, place them in some kind of rust-proof container – a large plastic colander, for instance – that lets the air circulate freely. Keep in a cool, airy place, but not a refrigerator. Then you'll find it quick and simple to peel potatoes as they're needed, to slice and sauté, or to cream with milk, butter and plenty of seasoning and re-heat in a well covered dish. Another way of using the pre-cooked potatoes is to slice them and use them to cover a casserole, topped with butter knobs and grated cheese.

More *potato* ideas? If you're jacket baking them, stand them in boiling water for 20 minutes beforehand. They'll be ready much quicker. New potatoes scrape easier if put into a bowl, covered with boiling water, and left 2 or 3 minutes.

When you need only small amounts of *apples*, *celery*, or *onion*, using dried flakes is quicker than preparation.

Tomatoes peel easily if put in boiling water for a few seconds. If you're only peeling one or two, hold them on a fork over a gas flame until the skin pops.

Mushrooms don't need peeling. Unless they're really filthy, just rinse them in cold water, and shake them in a dry cloth to get rid of the moisture. Remember that small mushrooms are delicious raw, in a salad, or on their own with French dressing.

Grow *mange tout* or *asparagus peas* in the garden. Picked when young, they only have to be tailed and cooked whole. Which saves lots of time. You can do this with ordinary peas, too, if they're very thin and young. Fabulous with a little butter.

JIFFY WAYS WITH FOOD

If you're serving chops or sausages, and haven't any time to make a gravy, heat up a can of *creamed sweet corn* to go with them. Or serve *canned tomato soup* flavoured with a little Worcester sauce and a pinch of extra salt and sugar.

A large pat of *flavoured butter* topping each portion of meat, fish, etc. is another sauce alternative. Allow about 2 oz. butter per person, and add to it ¼ tsp. made mustard; *or* chopped parsley, lemon juice and black pepper; *or* plain lemon juice; *or* curry powder and a few sultanas.

Yoghurt makes a good sauce replacement if you're serving white fish. Just spoon it over the fish before baking in a slow oven.

If you've a few moments to knock up a quick sauce, try one of these:

Mushroom Sauce: Heat 1 can condensed cream of mushroom soup with 1 oz. butter, 3 tbsp. cooking sherry or milk. When warm, add 2 oz. grated Cheddar, or 1 oz. Parmesan and a pinch of cayenne pepper. Serve on cod steaks, lamb chops, hamburgers.

Cream Curry Sauce: Sauté half a green, chopped pepper in a little butter. Add 1 can cream of chicken condensed soup, ½ tsp. curry powder, and a dash of Tabasco. Serve over sliced hard-boiled eggs, or pour over stuffed pancakes.

Cheese Sauce: Melt about 8 oz. of creamy processed cheese spread, and pour this over cauliflower, or mix with cooked macaroni.

Tomato Sauce: Heat can of condensed tomato soup, add a little tomato ketchup and vinegar, and blend.

Tartare Sauce: Allow 1 dstsp. sandwich spread to 1 cup mayonnaise. Chill, and serve with fish dishes.

Soups

Soup makes a good satisfying meal on a cold day, but useful as packet and canned varieties are, they haven't got quite the flavour of the real home brew. Still, you can do all sorts of things to make them more of a meal.

For instance, you can thickly butter a large slice of crustless bread per person, and put the slices side by side on a baking tray.

Sprinkle finely grated cheese over them, and bake at Gas Mark 4, 350°F., for about 40 minutes. Meanwhile, heat your favourite thick soup; when it's poured hot into the bowls, float a cheesy bread slice (whole or cubed) on each helping.

Crisps

Worth a section on their own, because of all their handy uses. Serve them hot, or as they are, with roast or fried chicken, instead of cooking potatoes. Scatter them over the top of a hotpot, or stew, immediately before serving. Crush them and lightly fold into mashed potatoes at the last moment. Crumble them and mix with sugar to sprinkle on top of a plain cake before baking. Break them up to serve on thick soups. Serve them with dips at parties, picnics, evening snacks. Crumble them in salads, alone or with an equal quantity of grated cheese. You can even use them to make a flan or tart casing, instead of pastry (see p. 234).

Vegetable Ideas

You want to dress up a vegetable, but you're short of time? *Peas* are pepped up by the addition of chopped fried bacon, or ham, and tiny cubes of fried bread. Coat cold *cauliflower* sprigs with mayonnaise, or hot cauliflower with a packet curry sauce. Toss *broad or runner beans* in French dressing, instead of in butter. Sprinkle sliced *carrots* with lemon juice and grated or finely chopped walnuts. Serve *brussels sprouts* with chunks of hot, cooked chestnut.

Baking

Maybe you need a tea-time cake and a lunch-time pudding, but haven't time for both. Try this, using a bought sponge sandwich, or one you've just made (see pp. 199 and 200).

For a cake, take one half of the sandwich, moisten it with fruit juice, cover with rows of fresh or canned fruits. Glaze it by brushing with melted apricot jam. Chill, and put on whipped cream before serving. Or, more economically, dust with caster sugar.

33

Cut the other cake half into wedges, arrange them in an oven-proof dish, and spoon over with stewed apples, rhubarb or plums. Sprinkle with cinnamon or mixed spice, dot with butter, and heat through in moderate oven (Gas Mark 4, 350°F.). Serve with vanilla ice cream, or with custard.

Fillers

There's always a day when you've only prepared a light meal, but the kids say they're ravenous . . . when they bring home a couple of friends you hadn't bargained for. Fillers can save the day.

For instance, if your *batter mix* is in store (see p. 43) it's the quickest thing in the world to bake a savoury Yorkshire pudding to go with whatever the main course is. If you want to dress the batter pudding up, cook it in a larger tin than usual so it comes out flatter. Then, when cooked, cut into squares, top with slices of fresh tomatoes or squashed up canned ones, slices of salami or other flavoursome sliced meats, and plenty of grated cheese. Brown under the grill and serve piping hot as *Pudding Pizza*.

Alternatively, the addition of a little sugar to your batter pudding means you can serve it as an extra 'afters' – hot and with syrup or jam.

Back to savoury fillers, a good helping of *potato* makes any meal seem larger, and *instant potato powder*, quickly reconstituted with milk or water the way the packet says, can be mashed into potato you've already cooked.

If a stew or soup is cooking, *dumplings* are speedily made and cooked in the tasty liquid, particularly if you've a container of *suet mix* handy. If you haven't time for that, bolster the dish with more water, and a stock cube, and a tin of whatever vegetables you have.

Any sort of meat, fish or chicken dish that's in a white sauce can be stretched by stirring in a few chopped, *hard-boiled eggs* – just long enough before serving to heat them through.

And did you know that two to four heaped tablespoons of *oatmeal*, stirred into a minced meat dish, and cooked with it, adds an extra serving, and takes on the flavour of the dish itself?

EMERGENCY ACTION

Do you start cooking, then realise you haven't got everything the recipe says? Or maybe you make a blunder, and want to salvage *something* from the wreck? There's not a remedy for everything, sadly – the time I mistakenly boiled a nugget of white soap along with nuggets of potato is a case in point – but sometimes emergency action saves the day.

If a recipe calls for *thick cream* for decoration, and you haven't any of the fresh sort, you can use a *can of cream* that's been chilled in the refrigerator for a day. Open it, without shaking, pour off the liquid or whey, and use the remaining thick cream for piping.

In place of each tablespoon of *cornflour* needed for thickening, you can use 2 *tbsp. plain flour*. For ½ *pint fresh milk*, substitute ¼ *pint evaporated milk and* ¼ *pint water*, well blended; or 2½ *heaped tbsp. instant non-fat milk powder stirred into* ½ *pint of cold water*.

Short of *eggs* for cake-making? Well, in place of two eggs, you can use *one egg and* 1 *tbsp. of vinegar*; or for each egg required over three, use an *extra tsp. baking powder*. In puddings, use *one egg and* 1 *dstsp. cornflour* in place of two eggs.

If you don't have any *browned breadcrumbs*, then *crushed crisps* usually act as an alternative; while *crushed cornflakes* can stand in for *crushed nuts* as a topping.

Instead of 1 *oz. of bar chocolate*, use 3 *tbsp. cocoa and* 1 *tbsp. butter*, and in place of *egg and breadcrumb* for coating use the *white of an egg*.

And if you must have a *piping bag* to ice a party cake prettily, make one out of greaseproof paper or, failing that, use the corner of a clean, strong envelope that's had its point snipped off.

If the *shell of an egg* cracks during boiling, a few drops of *added vinegar* helps to prevent the contents overflowing into the water.

Most unsatisfactorily baked *cakes and biscuits* can be crushed up and used as *sweet toppings* for stewed fruits.

Sometimes dishes don't turn out in flavour quite the way intended. A common fault is having *soup or stew too salty*. If that happens, try putting in a large *peeled potato*, and continue cooking it for a while.

With any luck, the potato will absorb the excess saltiness – remove it before serving.

Too-hot curry? There's little can be done it it's really fiery. But if it's just a little too warm for children's tastes, tone it down by adding some tomato sauce, a teaspoon of sugar, and the juice of half a lemon.

TEMPER-SAVING TIPS

It's the little hold-ups and hang-ups that make the best of us somewhat snappish when we're cooking, and in a rush. So here are a few points worth bearing in mind.

Hard-boiled eggs slice easier if you do the job with a wet knife. *Scrambled eggs* are lighter and fluffier if you add a pinch of baking powder, or ½ tsp. cornflour per egg, with a little milk. *Fried eggs* won't stick or break in the pan if you add a teaspoon of flour to the fat before frying.

Fried bread will be crisp, not soggy, if each slice is spread on both sides with butter or margarine then fried in a dry pan until golden brown.

Frying that's smelly or leads to burn-ups is aggravating and often wasteful. When deep frying, remember that 375°F. is the ideal temperature. If you haven't a thermometer, drop a one-inch cube of stale bread in the fat. The cube should – if the fat's just right – sink to the bottom, then rise to the surface immediately, turning golden brown in a minute. If it sinks and stays sunk, the fat isn't hot enough. If the oil smokes, and the bread goes dark brown, then the fat is *too* hot.

Something that really banishes the smell of frying is using the oven instead of the stove top. Put about ¼ inch of cooking oil into a baking tin, and put it for 10 to 15 minutes into the centre of a pre-heated, moderately hot oven. Put the food that you've coated or prepared as usual into the tin, and baste it with the hot fat. Cook till tender. Drain, and serve.

Sausages dipped in boiling water before frying, are less susceptible to bursting.

A joint of meat carves more easily and economically if you allow it to stand for five minutes after it comes out of the oven. When completely cold, it carves even more readily and thinly.

Parsley chops quickest if you either have a special mincer for it, or put it into a small china basin and then snip it with scissors.

Rice stays whiter, and the grains separate, if you add a teaspoon of lemon juice to the cooking water.

Stews and soups with a nasty surface layer of fat lose this if you lay a piece of absorbent paper over the top.

Cabbage smells less strongly as it cooks if you add a teaspoon of lemon juice, or the tiniest piece of soda, or a little sugar, to the water.

Gravies and sauces cooked ahead of time won't be veiled with a skin if, before you leave them to stand, you press a piece of oiled or wet greaseproof paper over the surface, then cover with the lid of the pan or with a plate. When you lift off the paper, the skin will come with it.

Onions that cause sore eyes and tears when you peel them are real temper-makers. Try holding a large slice of bread between your teeth as you chop them, to absorb the vapour. Or peel them under water. One or t'other *might* work!

Vegetables won't over-boil so easily if you add a small knob of butter to the water.

Instant skim-milk powder has rescued me from disaster time and time again, and it isn't as noticeable in flavour as evaporated milk. For drinks, I prefer to make it up by the pint (as instructed on the tin or packet) rather than sprinkling it on the surface. Made up in a jug, it's ready for cooking, too. White sauces, and milk puddings all work out cheaper if you use milk powder instead of fresh milk. And yoghurt made with skim milk powder is just as good as if it's made with fresh milk. One firm selling an excellent yoghurt making electric 'incubator' also sells skim milk in bulk at greatly reduced prices. (Details from The Shaw GB Partnership, 2 Admirals Road, Park Gate, Near Southampton, Hants.)

Whipping cream insufficient? Stretch it to its limits – and make it lighter and fluffier, too – by adding the white of an egg before whisking.

Custard won't acquire a skin if you've made it with demerara sugar, or if you sprinkle it with sugar while still hot, and cover immediately with a saucer or plate.

Treacle goes further, mixes better, if it's warmed. Same goes for golden syrup.

If you're making *cakes*, and are short of tins the same size, mould foil (double thickness) round the outside of the cake tin whose measurements you want to reproduce. Once sure there are no gaps, carefully remove the foil case, and use this as your baking tin.

READY-MIXES

For years, every time I had a baking session I started from scratch. Then I discovered I'd be far better off by making certain mixtures in bulk – up to a certain stage – and drawing on them as I needed them. It took a while to acquire several large-size lidded containers to store the mixes, but was well worth the investment because of the long term saving in time. A saving in money, too, if you consider that without your own mixes you might resort hurriedly to more expensive packets, or bought foodstuffs.

The mixes on the following pages include ones for different

kinds of sweet and savoury baking, and for puddings. After these come a miscellany of sauces, dressings, sweet toppings and others. All of which will save time over weeks ahead, if you prepare them in advance.

After each bulk mix, I've listed the names and page numbers of recipes in which it's used. And you'll probably discover for yourself variations on the basic ideas, and use them to speed up your own favourite recipes.

Shortcrust Pastry Mix
(For making plain, sweet or cheese shortcrust. Also for making crumble.)

> 8 *cups plain flour*
> 12 *oz. lard or good shortening, or a half and half mixture of shortening and margarine*
> 2 *level tbsp. caster sugar* (it won't taste sweet, but helps the general flavour)
> 2 *level tsp. each of salt, baking powder and cream of tartar*

Put dry ingredients into a good-size mixing bowl. Cut fat into little pieces, and work it in with fingertips till the mixture is like breadcrumbs. Store in a tight lidded plastic container in refrigerator or cool larder, where it should keep several weeks. Roll out and use in the ordinary way.

TO MAKE SHORTCRUST
Mix with cold water to a soft dough, allowing about 2 tbsp. water to each 2 cups of the mix.

TO MAKE SWEETENED SHORTCRUST
To each 2 cups Pastry Mix, add 3 tbsp. caster sugar, and mix to a soft dough with 2½ to 3 tbsp. cold milk or an egg (if necessary, add a little more milk, egg, or cold water).

TO MAKE CHEESE PASTRY
For every 2 cups of mix, add 6 heaped tbsp. strong flavour

grated cheese, a pinch of cayenne, 2 tbsp. cold milk, and 1 beaten egg.

TO MAKE CRUMBLE TOPPING
To 2 cups of mix, add 3 tbsp. brown sugar.

A GUIDE TO QUANTITIES
A lot depends on how thickly or thinly you like to roll your pastry, but here are some general quantities. For instance, to make a 10", open topped tart or flan you need 2 cups of Pastry Mix. To make the above, plus a 'lid' of pastry, allow $3\frac{1}{2}$ cups Pastry Mix. For a 'lid' for a deep dish (approx. 8" × 11" × 3") family meat or fruit pie, use $1\frac{1}{2}$ to 2 cups, or if you want to line the pie dish with pastry as well, reckon on about 4 to $4\frac{1}{2}$ cups Pastry Mix.

Pastry Mix can be used in the following recipes: Cold Chicken Pie (p. 76); Bacon and Egg Flan (p. 70); Veal and Lemon Flan (p. 80); Caraway Crunchies (p. 205); Cheese and Sultana Flan (p. 167); Crumble Puddings (p. 163); Apple Cheese Crumble (p. 140); Pear and Apricot Crumble (p. 141).

And you'll find more, different, pastry recipes and ideas on pp. 230 - 233.

Suet Mix
(For making, puddings, pastry, or dumplings.)

> 6 *cups S.R. flour*
> 3 *cups shredded suet*
> $\frac{3}{4}$ *tsp. salt*

Mix well together, then keep the mixture in a tightly lidded container in a refrigerator or cool place, to use as required.

Use it for making your favourite conventional puds and pies, or for any of these recipes: Sausage Pizza (p. 94); Cheese and Bacon Slices (p. 109); Coffee Kisses (p. 174); Apple In-and-Out (p. 138); Tangy Treacle Tart (p. 139); Fruity Poly (p. 139); Cherry Dumplings (p. 140); Apricot Dumplings (p. 140).

GUIDE TO MIXING AND QUANTITIES

For suet dumplings, 2½ cups of Suet Mix with about 6–7 tbsp. water makes 12 small or 6 large dumplings. Cook 15 minutes or longer, depending on size. To make suet pastry, mix as for dumplings then roll out on a well floured surface and bake as ordinary pastry. Incidentally, suet crust pastry is deliciously crisp yet not hard, and I find it easier to roll out than ordinary pastry since it doesn't break so easily. If, when you're making up the mix, you need more water add it only drops at a time, until the mixture holds together in a firm, soft but not sticky dough that comes cleanly away from your hands.

Note: For pastry, you can use plain flour instead of self raising, if you prefer, but this isn't so good for dumplings.

Bake Mix
(For cakes, puddings, scones.)

> 1 *lb. soft margarine*
> 2½ *cups caster sugar*
> 4 *large eggs (or 5 standard)*

Beat the soft margarine with a wooden spoon, then gradually beat in the sugar, till the mixture is light and fluffy. Break eggs into another basin and beat together till completely blended. Gradually add this to the margarine and sugar mixture, till the whole is fluffy and well blended. If you haven't an electric hand or stand mixer, you may find it easier to mix the Bake Mix half quantities at a time, finally blending the two halves together.

Put the final, fluffy mixture into a container, cover, and keep for up to 2 weeks in a cool place (not a refrigerator unless the weather is very hot, though if you do need to it's fine, providing you beat it up a bit more before using). If you've a home freezer, divide the mixture into equal amounts (5 rounded tbsp. per portion is probably fairly convenient) and store in sealed containers till required.

Once prepared, you can use your Bake Mix for Crisped Coffee Cake (p. 204), Mincemeat Topper (p. 204), Cocoa Cake (p. 203), Crunchy Topped Squares, (p. 202), Scones (p. 201), Family Loaf

Cake (p. 222), Steamed Sponge Pudding (p. 162), Sweet Fillings for Pastry Cases (p. 141), Assorted Jiffy Buns (p. 207), Simple Sponge (p. 200).

Basic Scone Mix

> 6 *cups S.R. flour*
> 1½ *level tsp. salt*
> 6 *oz. margarine*

Sift flour and salt together, into bowl. Add margarine, cut into small pieces. Rub with fingertips till you have a fine, breadcrumb-like mixture. Store in a covered container, in a refrigerator or other cool place. Then use it as needed to make not only Scones (p. 202), but also Veal Cobbler (p. 78); Liver Slices (p. 85); Banana Honey Buns (p. 206); Date Loaf (p. 205); Quick Pizzas (p. 189); Savoury Drop Scones (p. 185); or Savoury Pinwheels (p. 171).

Keeping Crumble

Once mixed, this keeps weeks in a refrigerator, though, if your family like crumble the way mine does, it won't have much chance to prove its keeping qualities!

> 12 *heaped tbsp. plain flour*
> 13 *oz. margarine or butter*
> 1½ *cups quick porridge oats*
> *good pinch salt*
> 6 *rounded tbsp. demerara sugar*

Rub together flour and margarine, then stir in the oats, salt and sugar till all are well blended. Keep in an airtight jar, and use to top canned fruit pie fillings, sprinkle on baked custards etc.

Unless the crumble is topping a slow cooking dish, in which case follow the recipe, it generally cooks best in a fairly hot oven (Gas Mark 6, 400°F.), taking ½ to ¾ hour.

Multi-purpose Mix

With this utterly basic dry mixture in a lidded container, in

a cool place, you'll be able to make cakes, biscuits and scones in
no time.

> 8 oz. margarine
> 6 cups S.R. flour

Rub the above together – it's as simple as that. Then store, and use
to make Scones (p. 201); Malted Loaf (p. 226); Apple and Almond
Fingers (p. 206); or to make other favourite recipes, adding appro-
priate ingredients.

Bulk Batter Mix

A dry mix that keeps for several weeks.

> 8 cups plain flour
> 10 tsp. cream of tartar
> 5 tsp. bicarbonate of soda
> 1 tsp. salt

Sift all ingredients together, then stir very well to ensure that they
are completely blended. Store in an airtight container.

To make a coating batter, for each 9 tbsp. Bulk Batter Mix
allow 1 small egg mixed with enough milk or water to make $\frac{1}{2}$ cup
liquid. Otherwise, follow these recipes: Drop Scones (p. 200);
Fritters, sweet and savoury (pp. 145, 185); Pancakes, sweet and
savoury (pp. 102, 143); Batter Pudding (p. 144); Fruit Batter
Pudding (p. 145); Rich Batter Pudding (p. 145); Sausage and Cheese
Toad (p. 94).

Streusel Topping

Kept in store, in a lidded container, this is always ready to sprinkle,
before baking, on any of the fruit cakes or fruit loaves in this book.
The result is an attractive, scrunchy surface.

> 4 level tbsp. plain flour
> 1$\frac{1}{2}$ oz. butter or margarine
> 2 rounded tbsp. demerara sugar

Rub all ingredients together. That's all.

Frothy Topping

Treat cans of evaporated milk this way, and you can always make an instant dessert.

Stand the tins of evaporated milk in water that comes up to their middles. Bring the water to the boil, then let it bubble gently for 25 minutes. Remove tins, and chill in the refrigerator for at least 24 hours. Whenever you want a creamy frothy topping, and don't want to lash out on real cream, open up a tin of your evap. and whip it till it comes up good and frothy. Or use the prepared evaporated milk to make the basic dessert on p. 127, which can be translated into all sorts of flavours.

Refrigerator Cream

You know how expensive real cream is, specially double cream? Well, here's a way of making it cheaply from nothing but your everyday pintas.

Let unopened bottles of milk stand in the fridge as long as possible, so that the cream settles thickly at the top. Then remove the cream (carefully pouring or using a little suction gadget obtainable from most good stores) and keep it in a lidded container in the fridge. Add to it over several days. When you want to use it, tip the stored cream into a bowl, and beat as you would for double cream. It will come up thick and delicious and almost double in bulk.

Vanilla Filling or Mock Cream

> 2 *rounded tbsp. cornflour*
> ½ *pint milk*
> 4 *tbsp. sugar*
> 2 *oz. margarine*
> ½ *tsp. vanilla essence*

Blend the cornflour with a little of the milk, then gradually stir in the rest of the milk till smooth. Bring this to boil over a gentle heat, stirring. Once it boils, simmer for a minute, then remove from the heat and leave to become cold. (A piece of slightly damp greaseproof paper on top prevents crust forming.) Beat the sugar and the margarine. Add the vanilla essence – can be less than ½ tsp. if you prefer. Add the cold cornflour mixture to the margarine and sugar mixture, beating it in a dessertspoon at a time till quite smooth. Having made this filling, store it in the refrigerator or cool place, covered with greased greaseproof, ready to use as quick cake filling, for sandwiching together plain biscuits as a tea-time treat, or sandwiching layers of puff pastry with jam etc.

Potato Dumpling Mix

This will keep several days in a covered container in the refrigerator, and you can use it to make Supper Quickie (p. 186); Potato Dumplings (p. 185); and Sweet Spud Dumplings (p. 163).

> 2 *lb. semolina*
> 4 *firm-packed cups cooked mashed potato*
> 4 *eggs*
> *a little salt*

Put semolina in bowl with potato; blend. Beat the eggs, then stir them well into the potato mixture till it's a smooth thick paste. Then it's ready to store or to use straightaway if you prefer. The amount above, incidentally, will make hearty portions for *two* meals for *six* people.

Cheese Mix

Handy for spreading on toast, then browning in oven or under grill; for putting on fried bread and topping with an egg. You can put it into a sandwich, too, with a slice of ham, and then fry or toast the sandwich. Or use it to make the cheese sauce needed for Egg Crisp (p. 92); Tuna Mornay (p. 97); and Celery au Gratin (p. 116); as well as for Speedy Rarebit (p. 185).

It keeps for weeks in a refrigerator, and here's how to make it:

> 6 *eggs*
> 3 *dstsp. dry mustard*

3 *tsp. Worcester sauce*
1¾ *pints milk or beer*
3 *lb. grated cheese (a strong Cheddar is ideal)*
3 *oz. butter or margarine*

Beat the eggs lightly, put into saucepan, and stir into it the mustard, sauce, liquid and cheese. Add the fat. Place over a medium heat and stir till the mixture thickens. At this stage, pour into a large container. Cover with a lid or with foil when cool.

FOR CHEESE SAUCE

Blend any measure of Cheese Mix with enough milk or stock to make the consistency needed (usually about ¼ of the amount of the Cheese Mix). Blend in a pan over low heat, stirring, till smooth and hot.

Tomato Butter

To spoon onto boiled potatoes, fish steaks, green beans, or anything else you fancy.

8 *oz. butter*
4 *tbsp. tomato purée*
salt and pepper
sprinkle of sugar to taste
dash of Worcester sauce

Gently heat the butter and tomato purée, stirring it to blend thoroughly. When hot and smooth, stir in seasonings. Keep in the refrigerator in a lidded jar or pot.

French Dressing

¼ *pint white vinegar*
¾ *pint corn oil*
2 *level tsp. caster sugar*
2 *level tsp. salt*

$\frac{1}{4}$ *level tsp. freshly ground black pepper*
2 *level tsp. French mustard*

Put all the ingredients into a jar, cover it and shake well. It stays good for weeks, but remember to shake the bottle each time before use.

Note: if seasonings aren't exactly to your taste, adjust them till they are. People vary tremendously in their opinions of what makes a 'good' dressing.

Milk Dressing

> 4 *tbsp. olive oil*
> 1 *tbsp. malt vinegar*
> 2 *tbsp. evaporated milk*
> *salt and pepper*
> 1 *level tsp. made mustard*
> 1 *tsp. lemon juice*
> 1 *tsp. Worcester sauce*

Measure all the ingredients into a screw topped jar. Shake well, before using.

Store Cupboard Mayonnaise

This couldn't-be-simpler mayonnaise keeps for ages, and costs far less than the shop-bought kind. Use it to cover hard-boiled eggs for egg mayonnaise (always a good, quick summer meal), to bind leftovers of fish or chicken for salads, to serve with salmon etc.

> 2 *egg yolks*
> 1 *tsp. salt*
> $\frac{1}{4}$ *tsp. pepper*
> 1 *tsp. dry mustard*
> 1 *tbsp. sugar (optional, but kids often like it)*
> $\frac{1}{4}$ *pint salad oil*

¼ *pint vinegar or bottled or fresh lemon juice (vinegar makes it
    longer lasting)*
1 *oz. margarine*
2½ *tbsp. plain flour*
8 *fluid oz. warm water*

Put yolks, seasoning, sugar, oil and vinegar into a bowl, without
stirring. Melt margarine in a saucepan. Remove from heat, and stir
in the plain flour. Slowly add warm water. When smooth, replace
over heat. Stir until mixture thickens and boils, then pour it
straight away onto ingredients in mixing bowl, and whisk whole
lot together like crazy. In moments, you'll have lovely creamy
mayonnaise.

Sweet Mayonnaise

1 *small can sweetened condensed milk*
¼ *pint olive oil*
¼ *pint distilled vinegar*
2 *egg yolks*
½ *level tsp. salt*
1 *level tsp. English mustard (dry)*
dash cayenne pepper

Whisk all ingredients until thick. Store in an airtight bottle in a
cool place, and use as required.

Make and Store Roux

The roux is the basic thickening for many sauces, and if you make
plenty, then divide it into portions and wrap in foil packets, it will
last a good time in refrigerator or freezer. When you're ready to
thicken sauces, stews, gravies and so on, just drop pieces of the
roux into the hot liquid, and stir until it bubbles and thickens.

1 *cup butter*
1½ *cups plain flour*

Melt butter and stir in flour. Cook gently, stirring, to make a white lump-free roux. If you want a brown roux, do the same but cook *very* slowly, till mixture becomes light brown (do this in a baking tin in a moderate oven, if you like). Use according to preference – but generally 3–4 level tbsp. roux to 1 pint liquid makes a thin sauce, while 6–8 level tbsp. to 1 pint makes a thicker one.

White Sauce

If you use white sauce often, as the basis of thick sauces, it's a good idea to make up a couple of pints of the stuff, and keep it in the refrigerator where it will last well for a few days. Make it either using your roux, or using cornflour and following the packet instructions. Quite apart from sauces, white sauce makes a useful binding ingredient for the fillings for savoury pancakes, flans and so on. And a baked potato is tasty if you scoop the potato from the skin, mix it with a well seasoned white sauce (or cheese sauce) and tinned shrimps.

Buttered Crumbs

They're nicer and cheaper than shop-sold dried crumbs, and store well.

All you do is melt 2 oz. butter in a saucepan, then add a 2 pint basin of fine white breadcrumbs. Let the crumbs soak up the fat, over a low heat, and stir the mixture gently from time to time. When all the fat is absorbed, spread the crumbs on baking sheets, and dry them in a very slow open (Gas Mark ½, 250°F.). When ready, they'll be creamy coloured and dry. Stored in a tightly lidded jar or plastic container, they'll keep fresh for 6–8 weeks, ready to use for dry coatings, or to be tossed with grated cheese (half Parmesan and half Cheddar is good) for other toppings.

TO USE THE CRUMBS AS A VEGETABLE TOPPING
Allow 2 oz. butter to each half-cup of dry crumbs. Melt the butter, and gently fry crumbs in it till golden. Serve sprinkled

over carrots, green beans, cauliflower etc. Or sprinkle on baked or grilled fish.

FOR SOFT CRUMBS IN RECIPES

Soak $\frac{1}{2}$ pint of the dried crumbs in 4–5 tbsp. hot water or milk for 5 or 6 minutes.

CHAPTER THREE

Healthy Eating

Feeding babies doesn't take too much moiling and toiling. All things being equal, so long as they have their milk, their strained or minced foods, and their cereal, cod liver oil and orange juice, we know they're O.K. Their weight, looks and bowels show us whether we're doing the right things, and if we're not a bit of juggling, and a word with the clinic or doctor, soon sorts matters out.

As the kids grow, though, it becomes trickier to keep them on the path of healthy eating. All too soon, they develop a taste for tooth-rotting things like boiled sweets and sticky toffee. Even if you keep sweets out of your own home, the start of school tends to undo all the good habits you've built up. And as they grow older, and are increasingly out of your sight, it becomes harder to keep tabs on what they stack away between meals.

Then, too, children develop all sorts of food fads and fancies. Teenage girls, specially, start worrying about weight when you can still almost see their ribs. Alternatively, if a child's on the big side, but leads an active sporting life and gets hungry quickly, just how much *should* you restrict his or her carbohydrate intake?

Before going any further, though, and without getting too involved, perhaps it will be useful to take a brief look at the nutrients we all need, and at the foods which contain them.

Protein comes from the Greek word meaning 'of first importance', which is just what protein foods are to our development. They build up new tissues during the growth of the body, and they repair damaged, broken down cells. First-class protein foods, as you probably know, are meat, fish, eggs, milk and cheese. Second-class protein ones are nuts, cereals (wheat, barley, oats) and pulses (peas, beans and lentils).

Fats are a highly concentrated source of fuel and energy. Sometimes mothers of plump children try to prevent them from having fats at all – butter, margarine and so on. But in fact, unless there's a definite medical reason for this, it can be a mistake. For fats actually help to burn up body fat. And a meal containing fat is more satisfying than one prepared without it – which means that a child will feel sustained for longer, and be less likely to turn for snacks to the biscuit tin or bread bin.

Remember two things about fats, though. One is that since they are hard to digest on their own, they should accompany some sort of carbohydrate food, in however small a quantity. The second point is not to forget that, in addition to the obvious fats, there are hidden ones like the fat in oily fish, in the yolk of egg, in cakes and pastries, peanut butter and so on. Because of this, it's often possible to cut down *excessive* fats while still keeping enough for the body's purposes.

Carbohydrates are almost entirely of vegetable origin. There are sugars (in fruits, sweets, honey, sweet vegetables, jams and syrups, milk and malted foods). And there are starches (all cereals, cereal products like flour and semolina, and foods made from cereal products such as bread, cakes, biscuits, pasta and so on.) Other foods are starchy in their own right – potatoes, rice, bananas. All of them are energy giving, but need to be used in a balanced way with other foods.

Vitamins are the next important thing to consider. These chemical substances, found in minute quantities in foodstuffs, are in practically everything to some degree. So, providing children have well planned, balanced meals, there should be no need to fly for bottles of vitamin tablets to supplement their diet.

Each different vitamin has its own particular function. *A* encourages health and development in children, and has other protective uses. It comes in carrots, in most orange, yellow and green fruits and vegetables, in meat, liver, kidney, oily fish, milk, cream, egg yolk, cheese, butter and vitaminised margarine. *D* is needed for teeth and bones, and comes in most of the Vitamin A sources –

animal fats, oily fish, egg yolk, milk, cheese, butter, vitaminised margarine. *E* is in wheat germ, milk, green vegetables, and water-cress; *K* in green vegetables. And various kinds of Vitamin *B* are found in whole grain cereals, wholemeal flour, yeast (and Marmite), liver, kidney, heart, lean meat, bacon, pulses, eggs, fish, milk (in a very small degree) and nuts.

And of course, there's Vitamin *C* for general health of body and skin, and to help in healing cuts and fractures. Children who eat a good amount of fresh green vegetables, citrus fruits, rosehips, black-currants and tomatoes will be getting a good supply of this vital vitamin.

Other substances like nicotinic acid, minerals, water and rough-age generally all take their place in a good mixed diet. And without getting too fraught about meal planning, a diet *will* be good and mixed if you include during the course of a day something from each of the groups above. Take a look, and you'll almost certainly find you *do*, even without thinking about it – so it's not as com-plicated as it might sound!

Do children need the same foods at different ages?

Starting at the small fry end of the scale, children from one to five are growing rapidly, and they need a really fine supply of body building foods. So at meal-times, keep an eye on their plate to see that essential foodstuffs are eaten *first* – the protein foods and vitamin-giving vegetables especially – while extra energy givers are offered at the end of the meal if still needed. Better no potatoes, or only a small one, with the main course, and a piece of bread and butter at the end of the meal, than a heap of potatoes or bread and butter with it which may cut his appetite and stop him from eating the more valuable foods. Apart from anything else, not falling into the habit of always having a carbohydrate with his meal when he's still in his high-chair, will make a child less tied to a pattern of hefty eating as he grows older. Same thing goes for introducing new flavours often. The child with masses of food fancies is often the one who's had a narrow, restricted diet during the early, forma-tive years.

From five to eleven, children are growing even more rapidly, and using up constant energy. Energy in sport, in learning, in coming to and from school, in play. They need a good mixed diet, with more energy-giving carbohydrates and fats than in pre-school days. And of course, they still need the body building and protective foods. Keep on introducing new ideas to them. And then maintain this pattern of well-balanced eating through their teen years.

Mind you, we're all entitled to one or two food hates. And where any of my children absolutely loathe something distinctively flavoured like liver, or heart, or spinach, I'm happy to let them skip these one or two things and to eat an alternative. But if food whims develop from nowhere, the rule of 'just a small helping' is a good one, and eventually the fad often disappears.

Certain things that children find difficult to take can be disguised. If eggs are a 'hate', a raw egg beaten into well-mashed potatoes, or used to thicken soups, isn't usually noticed. Whip eggs, too, into fruit flavoured milk shakes, and put them into puddings. The same thing goes for milk; if your child doesn't like drinking it by the glass, hot or cold, he *may* like a chocolate flavoured rice pudding, or custard with fruit purée – or good old flavoured milk shakes.

Lots of parents whose children don't like milk, hail the fact that they will take it on cereals. But remember that carbohydratey cereals – specially the sugar coated kinds – are things to go easy on. Because these are precisely the soft, over-refined carbohydrate foods that we *can* do without. A small helping is fine. Two or three large bowlfuls a day – not so good.

Perhaps this is a good moment to put in a word about carbohydrates. As pointed out, they are needed to a degree for energy, specially by growing children. Equally, too many can be harmful if a child is overweight. Also, it's carbohydrate foods – both the sugary and the starchy – that are so bad for teeth.

The fact that so many children today suffer from dental ailments is almost certainly a reflection on a way of life in which we overload ourselves with things like sweetened cereals, sugary fruit squashes and other drinks, and rich biscuits and cakes. It's almost certainly no coincidence that nearly all children under 12 suffer from dental decay in various degrees. The General Dental Council, which reported this fact, also said that if the trend continues, 25 per cent of all today's five year olds will need at least partial dentures before they're 20. And already 90,000 boys and girls are fitted with dentures each year.

Now, this doesn't mean banishing carbohydrates completely (unless, of course, a doctor recommends this for your child for a medical reason). But it does mean limiting them. You'll find recipes in this book for desserts like pancakes, for stew additions like dumplings, and for cakes. But it's up to you to use your discretion how and when to serve them.

A meal of stew with dumplings and potatoes, followed by pancakes with syrup, followed by a cup of sweetened tea and a slice of cake, is obviously not going to do any child much good. But have dumplings *or* potatoes, make dessert that day fresh fruit or give him cheese and celery, and forget the tea and cake altogether – and the youngster's whole eating pattern will be improved. It's that important thing *balance* again.

It makes sense, too, to consider what a child's eaten at school during the day, when deciding what to serve him in the evening. If lunch has been fish and chips, the evening meal could be something fresh and satisfying like ham and a tomato salad. If he's had a cold meal midday, with little protein, then something like liver and bacon, or an egg and cheese dish would go down well at night. If the midday dessert has been chocolate sponge and custard, tinned or fresh fruit would be a logical choice for the evening.

Is a bread and butter and cake tea ever good enough? The answer for a growing school child is honestly 'No' – particularly if breakfast is only toast and cereal in which case a child would be going 24 hours from one protein meal to the next. If a child has a proper midday meal at school, then the evening one needn't be elaborate. Scrambled eggs, or fish fingers with salad is fine. So is a hunk of cheese and an orange. However, if sandwiches make up his midday meal, at night he needs a proper meal.

The important thing is not to think that because a child has lunch at school, this is all he needs in the way of nourishment during the day. And I've put this in bold print because a series of interviews I conducted showed that many parents do believe just this. But in fact, all a school meal is intended to provide is one-third of the child's daily food needs. This being so, the necessity for a good evening meal and a satisfying breakfast becomes clear. As for breakfast there's nothing more nourishing and sustaining than bacon and eggs. Though if a child doesn't want this or any other cooked breakfast, a piece of cheese or a slice of ham with his toast, is infinitely better than toast and cereal alone. A cold meal contains the same protein as a hot, after all, and it's the protein that gives a bumper start to the day.

The same rules of selection should be applied to packed lunches, too. These needn't mean fillings slapped between slices of carbohydrate. School children can easily tote mini-meals to school in their lunch boxes. Salads can be taken in a container – lettuce, cucumber and tomato; celery and sultana; diced apple, nuts and lettuce; tomatoes and chopped chives. And to go with the salad, cold slices of meat off the joint, salami, ham or luncheon meat, or a piece of leftover cooked chicken are all tasty and nourishing. Or how about a slice or two of the Terrine on p. 164? As cheaper alternatives to cold meats, there are cheese chunks, hard boiled eggs, or tinned sardines or tuna. And in the winter, a wide-mouthed short thermos flask can contain a meat and vegetable stew, or thick nourishing soup. As for dessert – fresh fruit, nuts and dried fruits, or perhaps a small bar of chocolate (reckoned by most dentists to be less bad for the teeth than most other sweets and biscuits).

Sensible food planning, then, is the starting point for healthy eating, but mothers sometimes worry over other health points concerning food. One bone of contention is the re-heating of leftovers. So perhaps I'd better dispose of this before you get to the recipes themselves and find that some of them *do* involve warming already cooked foods! So long as ingredients used originally were good and fresh, dieticians generally agree that there's no harm in re-heating them, though certain rules improve both their flavour and nourishment value.

First, any re-heated food is best served in, or with, a sauce to avoid dryness. The food should be cut or minced finely, so that the heat can penetrate quickly and healthily – use a very hot oven, or deep fry. Finally, because some nutrients – specially Vitamin C – are lost by re-heating, serve these foods with something *fresh* which will make up for any lost nourishment. For instance, rissoles made with leftover joint meat could be topped with a slice of cheese melted under the grill, served with fresh green vegetables or grilled tomatoes.

The same thing goes for canned, packet, or frozen foods. Used occasionally, they are allies to any busy mother. But no meal should be made up entirely from convenience foods. A canned vegetable needs a fresh main dish served with it, and vice versa.

Finally, don't forget that though it may be convenient – it's bad for children to eat their meals crouched low around a television set; jaws munching, palates hardly conscious of the flavour or texture of what they're piling in their mouths. By sitting properly at a table, TV set switched off, they'll have improved digestions and take greater pleasure in what they're eating. What's more, they may actually spare time for a spot of conversation. All of which will help them towards good eating and good social habits when the time comes for them to lead their own lives.

CHAPTER FOUR

Main Meals

BEEF DISHES

Quick Casserole

A dish that you can prepare in about 10 minutes then forget while you go out to do the shopping, or to a school concert.

> $1\frac{1}{2}$ *lb. stewing beef*
> 3 *onions, chopped*
> 2 *tbsp. seasoned flour*
> 1 *meat bouillon cube*
> $\frac{1}{2}$ *pint boiling water*

Cut steak into cubes, and put into a casserole dish with the chopped onion. Sprinkle with the seasoned flour. Melt the meat bouillon cube in the boiling water and tip over meat. Cover with lid and place in the centre of a moderate oven, Gas Mark 4, 350°F. Cook for about $3\frac{1}{2}$ hours.

Pot Roast

> 3 *lb. piece of beef* (*top rib or fresh brisket*)
> 2 *tbsp. oil*
> 1 *lb. fresh tomatoes, skinned*
> *seasoning*
> *marjoram, bay leaf, crushed garlic*
> $\frac{1}{4}$ *pint stock or water*

Brown meat on both sides in hot oil in thick pan. Add skinned tomatoes and other ingredients. Cover pan tightly and simmer very slowly over gentle heat on top of the stove. Turn meat over once or twice during cooking. 2½–3 hours, depending on quality of meat.

Greek Pot Roast

When we were living in Cyprus, Gardeena, a lovely Turkish lady, taught me to do a pot roast this way.

> 3 *lb. piece of pot-roast beef*
> 2 *oz. butter*
> 2 *medium onions*
> 1 *lb. carrots*
> 1 *lb. runner beans*
> 2 *tsp. mixed herbs – or more of fresh*
> *medium* (15 *oz. or near*) *can of tomatoes*
> 1 *cup beef stock* (*made with a bouillon cube*)

Melt the butter in a deep, large pan (a good enough size to take all the meat and vegetables). Put in the meat joint, and turn it to brown all the sides. When coloured, remove and brown the sliced onions, and peeled carrots. Return meat to pan, cover the vegetables with water or stock and add a further knob of butter if most of the fat has been absorbed. Bring to the bubble, and simmer till all the water has evaporated, and only the butter remains. At this point, tip in the can of tomatoes and add the herbs. Bring back to simmering point, and continue to cook slowly, covered, till it has been on 1½ hours. Then add 1 lb. fresh, thinly sliced runner beans and simmer for a further ½ hour. (Add a little extra stock, or water, if needed.) By this time the meat should be tender, and the beaus cooked.

Bumper Beef Pot

> 2 *lb. stewing steak*
> 6 *rashers streaky bacon*
> 2 *medium onions*

2 leeks
2 oz. butter
1 rounded tbsp. flour
3 cups stock
½ lb. mushrooms
salt, pepper, bay leaf, chopped parsley
1 clove garlic, crushed

Cut beef into pieces, trimming off excess fat, but remembering that leaving some helps the flavour. Remove bacon rind and roughly cut. Peel and slice onions; wash leeks and slice horizontally. Melt butter in a saucepan and add the meat, onions and leeks. Fry for about 5 minutes, stirring occasionally to brown and seal the juices. Sprinkle flour over and stir thoroughly till meat is coated. Add stock and bring to the boil. Add seasonings and parsley to taste, cover pan, and simmer for almost 2 hours. During this simmering time, wash and slice the mushrooms (don't take off their skins, it's a time-waster and removes some of the flavour). Add these to the beef and cook another quarter of an hour. Taste, add extra seasonings if necessary, and serve.

N.B. providing your kids like it, a cup of red wine added to this, and/or a few caraway seeds gives the Beef Pot extra 'zing'.

Crusty Beef Carbonnade

2 lb. stewing beef (or chuck steak)
1 oz. seasoned flour
1 oz. dripping
2 large onions, sliced
1 clove garlic, crushed
6 oz. mushrooms, sliced
½ pint brown ale
1 pint water
salt, pepper, pinch of nutmeg
1 dstsp. vinegar
1 inch thick slices from a French stick
3 tsp. French mustard

Cut meat into 2 inch cubes and toss in flour. Melt dripping in a pan and quickly brown meat. Remove to a 3 pint ovenproof dish. Fry onions and garlic together for 5 minutes in the pan. Add mushrooms and stir in any remaining flour; add ale and water. Bring to the boil, stirring, and add salt, pepper, nutmeg and vinegar. Pour over meat, cover, and bake at Gas Mark 3, 325°F., for 2 hours. Skim any fat from casserole, pour it over the slices of bread, then spread the slices thickly with mustard and push them well down into the carbonnade, mustard side uppermost. Cook uncovered for a further 1 hour, by which time the bread will have floated to the top and become crispy.

Vinegared Beef

> 3 dstsp. vinegar
> 3 dstsp. oil
> salt and pepper
> ½ chopped onion
> ½ chopped garlic clove
> 6 slices cold roast beef
> 2 dstsp. soft butter
> ¼ cup tomato purée
> 1 tsp. lemon juice

Combine vinegar, oil, salt and pepper to taste, onion and garlic. Marinade beef slices in this for 2 hours upwards, turning meat several times. Combine butter, tomato purée and lemon juice. Put beef plus its marinade in shallow casserole; add butter mixture and cook, till it reaches bubbling point, in a moderate oven (Gas Mark 5, 375°F.). Serve with hot crusty bread.

Aloyau

A Breton meal that makes use of leftover joint, and store cupboard tins.

> 6 thick slices cold cooked meat (any kind)
> 2 cans drained haricot beans

about ½ lb. small white onions, cooked (or use the frozen sort)
1 cup cider
salt and pepper
½ cup chopped fresh parsley

Combine first three ingredients in a buttered casserole dish. Season to taste, pour over the cider, and heat to boiling in a moderate oven (Gas Mark 5, 375°F.). Sprinkle with parsley, and serve with French bread and wine.

All-day Wrap-Roast

Most of us cook a roast fairly quickly at a highish oven temperature. But it can be left to cook quietly all day, along with its vegetables. Then, when you're ready to eat at night – all that's left to make is the gravy. Whatever kind of joint you're roasting, wrap it in aluminium foil, with the edges tightly sealed. Stand the wrapped joint on a rack from the grill pan, or on something else that will allow the hot air to move around it. About 30 minutes before eating, remove foil – being careful to keep all juices for the gravy – and leave the joint to brown, which it won't have been able to do in the foil. Cook at lowest possible oven setting for about 7 hours – even left longer, it won't hurt.

Serve with buttered carrots and potatoes (see p. 117) cooked in the oven for the same time. Apple Almond Pudding (p. 158) can also be oven-cooked all day at lowest setting.

MEALS FROM MINCE

Speed Balls

1 lb. minced lamb
½ cup breadcrumbs (hard or soft)
½ cup milk
1 packet onion soup mix
1 cup water
approx. 1 oz. butter

Mix the minced meat, breadcrumbs and milk, shape into small balls, and brown in butter. Next, blend the packet of onion soup mix with the water and stir this into the butter and juices – *gently*, so meat balls don't break. Simmer for about 15 minutes. Serve on rice.

Meat Balls Mexicana

FOR MEAT BALLS
> 2 *cups porridge oats*
> 1½ *lb. minced beef*
> 1 *stock cube dissolved in ½ pint boiling water*
> 3 *tbsp. tomato purée*
> 2 *small onions, chopped*
> 1 *clove garlic, chopped*
> *seasoning*
> 1 *tsp. Worcester sauce*
> *seasoned flour and cooking oil*

Combine all ingredients and shape to form 12 meat balls. Roll in seasoned flour, then brown in just enough oil to cover bottom of pan.

FOR SAUCE
> 2 *small onions finely chopped*
> 15 *oz. can peeled tomatoes*
> 7 *oz. can whole kernel corn*
> 1 *tsp. paprika, ½ tsp. of cayenne (optional)*
> *seasoning*

Combine all sauce ingredients, and pour over balls. Cover and simmer 25 minutes.

Meat Balls and Rice Hot Pot

A store cupboard dish – all you need fresh is the minced beef, and even that could come from freezer or freezer compartment of

fridge if you have one. Good thing about this meal is that once in
the oven you can leave it quite alone for $1\frac{1}{2}$ hours without even a
stir, and that vegetables, meat and rice all cook in one easily-washed
casserole.

> $1\frac{1}{2}$ *lb. minced beef or lamb*
> $1\frac{1}{2}$ *cups long grain rice*
> 1 *medium can sliced, drained carrots*
> 1 *large can tomatoes (1 lb. 14 oz.)*
> 1 *heaped tbsp. dried onion flakes (or 1 large fresh chopped onion)*
> $\frac{1}{2}$ *level tbsp. basil*
> $\frac{1}{2}$ *level tbsp. mixed herbs*
> $\frac{1}{2}$ *tsp. sweet paprika, salt and pepper*
> *lemon juice*
> 1 *pint beef stock, made with bouillon cube*

Put rice at bottom of a large, well-greased casserole dish. In a bowl
stir together carrots, tomatoes (including the juice), onions, basil,
squeeze of lemon juice, and salt and pepper to taste. Pour this over
the rice. Work mixed herbs, paprika, a little lemon juice and salt
and pepper to taste, into the minced meat, then shape into about 18
balls. Put these on the rice mixture, and pour the beef stock over
everything. Don't stir. Cover with lid, and cook in centre of a preheated moderate oven (Gas Mark 4, 350°F.) for about $1\frac{1}{2}$ hours, or
till the rice has cooked and absorbed all the lovely juices, and the
meat balls are browned and tasty.

Oriental Meat Balls

> $1\frac{1}{2}$ *lb. minced pork*
> 2 *tbsp. soy sauce*
> $\frac{1}{4}$ *cup water*
> 1 *dstsp. powdered ginger (or more to taste)*
> 1 *crushed garlic clove*
> *salt and pepper to taste*
> *a little fat*

Mix everything to make little balls about an inch in diameter. Put in roasting tin, with a little fat, and bake uncovered for an hour in a fairly cool oven (Gas Mark 1 or 275°F.). Serve hot with a favourite sauce or gravy, and with cooked buttered noodles, mashed potatoes or rice.

Swiss Loaf

2 lb. minced beef
1½ cups diced Gruyère cheese
2 beaten eggs
½ chopped onion
½ cup chopped green pepper
1 tsp. salt, ½ tsp. pepper, 1 tsp. celery salt
½ tsp. paprika
2½ cups milk
1 cup dry breadcrumbs

Mix all together, put into a greased loaf tin and bake uncovered for 1½ hours at Gas Mark 3 or 340°F.

Crispy Beef Rolls

FOR ROLLS
1½ lb. raw minced beef
1 pint packet mushroom soup mix
salt and pepper to taste
6 tbsp. water
12 large thin slices white bread
2 oz. butter, melted
chopped parsley

FOR TOMATO SAUCE
2 oz. butter
2 oz. flour
2 beef stock cubes dissolved in ½ pint water
15 oz. can tomatoes

65

2 *tbsp. tomato ketchup*
½ *level tsp. oregano, salt and pepper*

Mix together minced beef, dry onion soup, salt and pepper. Blend in water. Remove crusts from bread. Divide mince into 12, and shape into rolls the same length as bread slices. Place rolls of mince along centre of bread slices then wrap bread round so that edges meet. Place on a baking sheet with the join underneath and brush with melted butter. Bake at Gas Mark 4 or 350°F. for 40–45 minutes until bread is crisp and golden brown.

For the tomato sauce, melt butter, stir in flour and cook for 2–3 minutes. Remove from heat and gradually stir in stock. Add tomatoes and juice, tomato ketchup and oregano. Return to heat, bring to boil and cook for 2 minutes stirring continuously. Reduce heat and simmer gently for 5 minutes. Season if necessary. Garnish each roll with a little finely chopped parsley. Hand tomato sauce separately.

Crisis Mince

Frankly, I've had lots of things far better than this, but several kids I know love it, and it does mean you can get lunch going in minutes.

1 *lb. raw minced beef*
1 *packet Knorr Minestrone soup*
1 *pint water*
2 *tbsp. tomato purée*
extra salt and pepper to taste

Plonk the beef, the minestrone soup mix and water into a saucepan, and stir till boiling. Simmer gently for 20 minutes, stirring occasionally. Serve on hot, boiled spaghetti, on real or instant mashed potato, or over toast topped with an egg. Refinements are to sprinkle with Parmesan cheese, and garnish with sliced stuffed olives.

Kids' Curry

The way lots of us like curry is hot and tear jerking. But some of our children and their friends don't feel the same way, though they do like the basic taste. So when I make curry for the kids, I make what they all call 'sweet curry'. It can either cook quickly on top of the stove, if you're late, or slowly in the oven if you want to come back to it after a 2–3 hours' shopping trip.

1½ *lb. minced beef or lamb*
2 *medium onions*
1 *clove garlic, crushed (optional)*
1 *medium can peeled tomatoes*
2 *tbsp. tomato purée*
1 *tbsp. coconut*
2 *tbsp. sultanas*
sprinkle of salt and black pepper
2 *tsp. brown sugar*
2 *tsp. curry powder*
2 *bay leaves*
1 *tbsp. lemon juice or vinegar*
2 *cups water, or stock made with bouillon cube*
cooking oil

Gently fry onion with garlic in oil, till golden and soft but not brown. Stir in the mince and cook that with the onion for about 10 minutes stirring occasionally. Mix curry powder with vinegar, brown sugar and tomato purée, and stir this into the mince and onion mixture. Then add all other ingredients, give a good stir, pour in water or stock, stir again, and leave to simmer in a lidded pan for 1 hour upwards. The longer you've time to leave it, the better the flavour. (If you prefer, once it's started to boil, put the curry in a tight-lidded dish in a slow oven, Gas Mark 2 or 300–325°F. when it can cook for 2–3 hours.) If necessary add a little more liquid.

This is equally good cooked one day and heated the next. Serve with fluffy boiled rice (see p. 103) and let them help themselves to little bowls of sliced tomato, chopped pineapple, desiccated coconut, chopped hard-boiled egg, sweet chutney, sliced banana, salted peanuts—whichever you can spare.

Note: For even speedier Mock Curry, heat 2 tins stewing steak in 1 tin Mulligatawny soup, with 1 tsp. each sugar and vinegar and 1 tbsp. tomato purée.

Cottage Loaf

> 2 slices bread, ½ inch thick
> ¼ pint milk
> 3 lb. minced lamb
> 2 tbsp. Worcester sauce
> 2 tbsp. tomato purée
> 4 tbsp. fruit chutney
> 2 rashers bacon, rind removed and diced
> 2 sticks celery, finely chopped
> 1 beef stock cube, crumbled
> 3 level tsp. salt
> freshly ground black pepper
> 3 lb. potatoes boiled and mashed with margarine and milk
> 1 tsp. cornflour

Soak bread in milk for ½ hour. Add all remaining ingredients except potato and cornflour and blend well. Place mixture in two 2 lb. loaf tins. Bake in preheated moderate oven, Gas 4, 360°F. on middle shelf for 1 hour. Drain off liquor. Turn out onto heatproof serving dish. Spread each loaf with hot creamed potato using prongs of fork to form 'thatched' effect. Return to oven for 25–30 minutes until golden brown, or brown under grill on low heat. Serve hot with gravy and garnished with parsley. To make gravy: Blend liquor with 1 level tsp. cornflour. Bring to boil, stirring continuously and cook for 1–2 minutes until thickened and clear.

Beef and Tomato Pie

> 1½ lb. minced beef
> 2 large onions
> 1½ lb. tomatoes
> 1 oz. bacon fat
> 1 tbsp. finely chopped parsley

pinch marjoram
2 tbsp. strong stock (can be made with bouillon cube)
2 oz. grated cheese
2 tbsp. dried breadcrumbs
salt and pepper
½ oz. butter

Finely chop onions and tomatoes. Heat fat in frying pan. Add onions and cook until soft. Mix in meat and cook over a high heat, stirring continually until meat is brown. Remove from the heat, stir in the parsley and marjoram, and season with salt and pepper. Arrange half the tomatoes in the bottom of a casserole; cover with the meat mixture and top with the remaining tomatoes. Pour over the stock. Sprinkle with the cheese and breadcrumbs, dot with butter and bake in fairly hot oven Gas Mark 5, 375°F. for about 1 hour or until meat is tender.

HAM, BACON AND CHICKEN

Ham with Honey Shallots

The honey gives a piquant flavour to this dish. And the ham can be as expensive or cheap a cut as you like (slices of boiled bacon could be substituted).

1 thick slice cooked ham per person
1 lb. shallots
1 cup vegetable stock, or water
3 tbsp. butter
2 tbsp. thick honey
salt and black pepper

Blanch shallots and cool slightly. Peel and brown them in butter. Heat a little of the stock in a heavy pan and add the honey, stirring well. Add shallots, rest of stock, and a shake each of salt and black pepper. Cover with a well fitting lid, and simmer 30 minutes stirring from time to time. If liquid reduces, add a few tablespoons more stock. About 10 minutes before serving, add ham slices, to heat through.

Bacon and Egg Flan

short pastry made with 2 cups Pastry Mix (see p. 39)
12 oz. chopped streaky bacon, crisply fried
1 pint milk
6 standard eggs
4 tbsp. grated cheese

Make pastry and roll thinly to line a 10 inch sandwich tin standing on baking sheet. Cover pastry base with bacon. Beat together milk, eggs, cheese and seasoning to taste, and pour this over the bacon. Bake at the centre of a Gas Mark 7, 450°F. oven, for 20 minutes then at Mark 3, 350°F. for a further 20–25 minutes. Garnish with parsley, mushrooms, or tomatoes.

Bacon and Apple Bake

4 large cooking apples
4 large Spanish onions
4 tbsp. flour
4 tbsp. brown sugar
1 cup chopped nuts
breadcrumbs
butter, water, nutmeg, salt and black pepper
6 rashers streaky bacon

Mix flour with about ¼ pint water to thin consistency. Add shake of salt and pepper. Peel and slice onions and apples; arrange in layers in a greased casserole as follows: onions, apples, bacon (first lightly fried), nuts and the flour-thickened liquid, adding a little seasoning and sugar to each layer. Top with breadcrumbs, dot with butter, and bake till tender. If needed add a little more water.

Chicory Rolls

> 6 *heads chicory*
> 6 *thin slices cooked ham*
> 2 *oz. margarine*
> *heaped tbsp. plain flour*
> ½ *pint milk*
> 6 *heaped tbsp. grated Cheddar cheese* (*strong*)
> ¼ *level tsp. mustard*
> *salt and pepper to taste*

TO PREPARE CHICORY

Wash chicory and remove any discoloured leaves. Place in large saucepan of boiling salted water. Boil 7–10 minutes until tender. Drain. Wrap a slice of ham round each head of chicory. Place the 'join' sides down, in a deep fireproof dish, and brush over the rolls with 1 oz. of the margarine melted.

TO MAKE SAUCE

Melt remaining ounce of margarine in small saucepan over a low heat. Stir in flour and cook until mixture bubbles. Add milk and bring to boil, stirring continuously. Cook 3 minutes, stirring all the time. Stir in 4 heaped tbsp. cheese, mustard and seasonings, and heat until melted, *but do not boil.* Pour sauce over the chicory. Sprinkle remaining cheese over. Bake on the second shelf from the top of fairly hot oven, Gas Mark 6, 380°F., for 20 minutes, until golden brown and heated through.

Country Bacon Bake

> 12 *oz. bacon*
> 1 *large onion, chopped*
> 6 *oz. mushrooms, sliced*
> 10 *large, thin slices white bread, de-crusted*
> 1½ *pints milk*
> 4 *large eggs, beaten*
> *salt and pepper*
> *margarine for frying and greasing dish*

Divide bacon into half, and chop one half. Fry chopped bacon with
onions and mushrooms until soft (about 3–4 minutes). Cut each
bread slice into quarters. Arrange half the bread in a buttered,
shallow 2½ pint ovenproof dish, sprinkle bacon mixture evenly over
bread, then arrange remaining bread and the whole pieces of bacon
on top. Warm milk, and pour onto eggs. Beat well, season and strain
over bread. Bake at Gas Mark 3, 325°F. for 50 minutes or until bread
is crisp and egg set.

Ham and Pineapple Pot

A creamy 'hash' that all incoming children seem to enjoy.

> 1½ lb. diced ham or boiled bacon (the kind you get on a cheap
>   hock is fine)
> 1¼ lb. potatoes, sliced
> 1 lb. can pineapple cubes
> 1 tbsp. flour
> salt and pepper
> 1 small packet frozen or canned peas
> 1 tsp. Worcester sauce
> 2 tbsp. oil for frying

Heat oil and lightly fry ham and potatoes for about 3 minutes.
Make pineapple juice up to 2 cups with water, and add to ham and
potatoes. Add seasonings, and simmer for 15 minutes. Mix flour
to smooth paste with 4 tbsp. water, and pour into ham mixture,
stirring and simmering for 3 more minutes. Add pineapple cubes,
and other things. Simmer 5 minutes.

Baked Ham

The 'paste' casing keeps in all the flavour. If you're really rushed,
follow recipe below, but wrap ham in foil instead of paste.

For any joint up to 4 lb. in weight, take 1 lb. flour and ½ pint
water. (For larger joints, increase the quantities of flour and water
in the same proportion.) Mix together to make a firm paste, knead

well until smooth. Put the weighed joint into a large pan, cover with cold water and bring to the boil gradually. Remove the joint and dry well. Roll out the paste on a floured surface, then enclose the joint in it and seal edges of the 'casing' well. Place with seal underneath, in a baking tin. Put 2 tbsp. water in the tin, and bake at Gas Mark 3, 330°F. allowing 30 minutes to the pound – though for joints less than 4 lb. in weight, give an extra 30 minutes. Before serving, remove paste from the joint, skin the ham, and while still warm coat with browned breadcrumbs.

Hammy Noodles

> 12 oz. noodles
> a couple of cups of ham pieces
> ½ lb. strong Cheddar cheese
> 1 green pepper
> 1 tsp. horseradish sauce
> 1 can condensed celery soup (or mushroom)
> ¼ cup milk
> 1 cup breadcrumbs
> salt and pepper
> butter

Cook noodles till tender. Mince together the ham, cheese and green pepper. Add to this the horseradish, soup and milk, plus salt and pepper to taste. Mix everything together, including cooked noodles. Bake, covered, in buttered casserole at Gas Mark 4, 350°F. for 40 minutes. Remove cover, sprinkle crumbs on top, dot with butter, and brown under grill.

(*Note:* You can do this with cooked chicken, or tuna pieces, too.)

Confident Chicken

So called because you've got to have enough confidence in this recipe to do just what it says – and nothing else. I'm not saying you *can't* add chopped green peppers, grated raw onion or whatever, but it's not necessary. You'll only waste time and bump up the cost.

Put into an ovenproof dish one chicken joint for each person. Tip over them condensed mushroom soup – one can for each 4 joints. Put on a tight fitting lid, and shove the dish in a preheated oven (Gas Mark 5, 375°F.). Cook for about 1 hour or till tender. Exact timing depends on thickness of joints. If your cooking preparations are rushed, but in *advance*, you can do the same thing using a whole chicken – two cans of soup if it's a large bird. In this case, have the oven at Gas Mark 1 or 275°F. and allow 3–4 hours for cooking, depending on size. Put giblets in the dish, too, if you like. Either way, the juices of the chicken blend with the creamy mushroom liquid and form the kind of scrumptious sauce that makes people say 'What's the recipe?' Don't tell them. Look mysterious as you serve it from a bed of rice. Hand vegetables separately – try tinned sweet corn kernels heated through at the last minute with a knob of butter, a dash of lemon juice and a sprinkle of pepper and salt.

Sister's Chicken

Boiling fowls aren't always easy to get, but most butchers can order them for you. And here's how to treat one for a summer salad meal that's prepared in advance.

Pot roast a boiling fowl with whatever vegetables are around. When tender take *all* the chicken off the bones, cut in fine strips and place in a mould or plain glass dish. Put carcass, bones and feet of chicken (if you're lucky enough to have them) in a pan with a sprinkle of salt and pepper, just cover with water, and bring to boil. Reduce heat, and simmer about an hour or till liquid has reduced by half. Strain and pour over sliced chicken. Put in refrigerator and it will set as a galantine that you can slice thinly. Delicious with a cucumber or cucumber and tomato salad.

Devilled Chicken

> 6 *chicken joints*
> 3 *tsp. cooking oil, salt*
> 3 *dstsp. vinegar*
> 1 *level tbsp. dry mustard*

2 tbsp. tomato purée
salt, pepper and (optional) a little garlic powder

Place chicken joints on foil, pour the 3 tsp. of oil over them, sprinkle on very little salt, then wrap in a loose 'parcel'. Cook in moderate oven Gas Mark 4, 350°F. for 45 minutes, till tender. Meanwhile blend all remaining ingredients. When chicken is tender, remove from oven and turn heat to Gas Mark 7, 450°F. Fold back foil, spoon the 'devilled' mixture over the chicken. Return to hot oven, uncovered, and cook about 20 more minutes basting occasionally. Serve on rice.

Chicken Hash

Use leftover chicken to make this dish – or cook the chicken purposely in advance, to use some for the hash, the rest for a salad, packed lunch or pilaf.

1 large can cream chicken soup
2 dstsp. butter
2 dstsp. minced onion
2 dstsp. minced parsley
¼ lb. button mushrooms, chopped (the canned kind will do)
salt and pepper
3 cups diced cold chicken
3 dstsp. sherry

Heat first 6 things to boiling, add chicken and heat to boiling again. Add sherry, correct seasoning, and serve.

Chicken Hawaii

1 large roasting chicken
4½ oz. can pineapple juice

Cut piece of foil large enough to enclose chicken, and lay the bird on this, on a meat tin or baking tray. (The chicken can be stuffed or not, as you like.) Pour the pineapple juice over and wrap the foil around to form a closed parcel. Cook approximately 35 minutes per pound at Gas Mark 7, 450°F. Open the foil for the last 15–20 minutes to complete browning. Remove the chicken to a hot serving dish, and use the juices in the foil to make a deliciously flavoured gravy.

Cold Chicken Pie

Extravagant, this, because you'll be lucky if it does more than six good servings. But delicious for a special occasion.

Joint two chickens (each about 3 lb.), remove the skin and bones, and then shred or chop the chicken meat. Hard boil 4–6 eggs. Line a deep pie dish with alternating layers of chicken, streaky bacon rashers, sliced onions, sliced mushrooms, chopped parsley and a little tarragon (if available). Season with a little salt and pepper as you go, but go easy on the salt, because of the bacon. Bury the hard-boiled eggs in this pie filling, cover the top with short crust (for quantity and method see p. 39), make a hole in the centre, and through this pour 3 tbsp. water mixed with 1 tbsp. soy sauce. Brush the pastry top with beaten egg, and bake the pie in a moderate oven (Gas Mark 4, 350°F.) for an hour and a half. Let it get quite cold before serving.

LAMB, VEAL AND PORK

Breast of Lamb with Eggs

A nourishing budget meal, with an unusual combination of texture and flavour.

> 2 *large, boned breasts of lamb*
> 6 *hard-boiled eggs, sliced thickly*
> 1 *packet stuffing mix (your favourite)*

Make stuffing according to directions, and spread it over the two breasts of lamb. Lay sliced eggs on top. Roll very firmly and tie or skewer. Weigh, and roast allowing 25 minutes per meat pound, plus an extra 25 minutes (Gas Mark 4, 350°F.).

Autumn Casserole

> 6 *lamb cutlets*
> 3 *small chopped onions*
> 1 *medium* (15 *oz.*) *can tomatoes*
> 6 *tbsp. finely chopped celery*
> *good pinch mixed herbs*
> 1 *tsp. sugar*
> *salt and pepper to taste*

Trim fat off cutlets, and place in casserole with everything else. Cover and place in moderate oven (Gas Mark 4, 350°F.) for about 1 hour or till chops are tender.

Pruned Lamb

A tasty way that makes the most of economy stewing lamb.

> 2 *lb. stewing lamb*
> 12–18 *prunes*
> 2 *medium onions*
> *salt and pepper*
> 1 *small tsp. marjoram*
> *juice of* 1 *lemon*
> 2 *cups water or stock*
> 1 *tbsp. flour*
> 1 *tsp. sugar*
> 2 *oz. butter or oil for frying*

Heat the fat in a large bottomed pan. Brown meat and put into casserole dish. Then brown the onions and add these to casserole. Sprinkle meat and onions with seasonings and lemon juice. To fats in pan, stir in 1 tbsp. flour and fry a minute or so. Add stock, bring to boil, stirring, then pour into casserole. Cook in a moderately hot oven (Gas Mark 6–7, 375–425°F.) for 1½ hours. Then add prunes and sugar. Cook for further ½ hour.

Layer Lamb Chops

> 6 *lamb chops*
> 1½ *lb. potatoes*
> ⅓ *cup evaporated milk*
> 2 *cooking apples, peeled and sliced*
> 4 *tsp. sugar*
> *salt and pepper to taste*

Grill lamb chops till some of the surplus fat has dripped away, and they are browned. Peel and slice potatoes, place them in a casserole dish, and sprinkle with salt and pepper. Pour evaporated milk (*not ordinary milk*) over potatoes; add the browned chops and sprinkle with salt and pepper. Spread the sliced apples over chops, sprinkle with sugar. Cover with lid, and put in fairly hot oven (Gas Mark 5, 375°F.) to cook for 1¾–2 hours.

Veal (or Pork) Noodles

> 2 *lb. stewing veal (or pie pork)*
> 1 *can condensed mushroom soup*
> 1 *onion finely chopped*
> 1 *large packet noodles*

Chop up pork or stewing veal pieces small, put with the chopped onion in a pan, cover with water and simmer till just tender. Then stir in the condensed mushroom soup, and when the liquid is back to bubbling, stir in noodles and cook a further 10–15 minutes till noodles are soft. Serve with green peas.

Veal Cobbler

Using a scone topping that's a change from pastry.

> 2 *lb. minced veal (cheapest stewing kind will do)*

2 *medium onions, peeled and chopped*
2 *oz. butter*
14 *oz. can tomatoes*
6 *oz. mushrooms, sliced*
salt, pepper and ½ *tsp. mixed dried herbs*

Make scones (using one of the methods on pp. 201 or 202) with an added 2 oz. grated cheese. Roll out scone dough and cut into rounds. Melt butter in heavy bottomed pan. Fry onion and veal in butter for 10 minutes. Add tomatoes, seasoning and mushrooms. When heated through, put into ovenproof dish. Arrange scones so that they overlap and cover the veal mixture. Brush them lightly over with milk or beaten egg, and bake at Gas Mark 6, 400°F. for about 30 minutes.

Paprika Veal

A meal that's spicy without being too much for younger children's palates.

2 *lb. stewing veal*
2 *oz. plain flour*
1 *level tsp. salt, pepper*
1 *level tbsp. sweet paprika*
2 *tbsp. cooking oil*
2 *onions, chopped*
1 *Oxo cube, dissolved in* ½ *pint hot water*
juice of ½ *lemon*
14 *oz. can tomatoes*
½ *level tsp. sage*

Trim excess fat from meat and cut into pieces. Put flour, seasoning and paprika into a polythene bag. Add meat and shake until it is well coated. Heat oil in a pan and lightly fry onions. Add meat and seasoned flour. Cook for a few minutes, stirring. Gradually stir in Oxo stock, bring to boil and cook for a few minutes. Add lemon juice, tomatoes and their juice, and seasonings. Turn into an ovenproof casserole dish, cover and cook in a very moderate oven (Gas Mark 3, 325°F.) for about 2 hours.

(*Note:* Be sure you use sweet, and not *hot* paprika).

Veal and Lemon Flan

If the pastry's prepared, and the veal minced, in advance, putting everything together takes little time.

PASTRY

> 3½ *cups Pastry Mix* (*p.* 39), *plus grated rind* ½ *lemon and* 1½ *tbsp. lemon juice in place of some of the water.*
>
> *Or* try this Easy Mix Pastry:
>
> 6 *oz. easy-mix shortening*
> 1½ *tbsp. lemon juice*
> 3 *tbsp. cold water*
> *grated rind* ½ *lemon*
> 12 *heaped tbsp. plain flour*
> ½ *level tsp. salt* (*sieved with flour*)

FILLING

> 1 *lb. minced pie veal*
> 2 *eggs beaten together*
> ½ *level tsp. mixed herbs, seasoning, beaten egg to glaze*

Make pastry using your Pastry Mix. *Or* put the shortening, lemon juice, water, grated lemon rind and 2 tbsp. flour and salt in a mixing bowl. Whisk with fork for ½ minute till well mixed. Add remaining flour, and stir till it's a firm dough. Roll out two-thirds of the pastry and line a 10 inch flan tin placed on baking sheet. Roll remaining pastry for the top.

To make the filling, mix together the minced meat and beaten eggs. Add herbs and seasoning. Place in pastry case. Damp edges of pastry lid and place it on top. Bake near the top of fairly hot oven (Gas Mark 6, 400°F.) for 35 minutes then reduce to Gas Mark 4, 360°F. for a further 30–35 minutes. Cover pastry with foil if it browns too much.

Somerset Pork

Just the thing to put in the oven before you go out, and find ready when you get back home.

> 3–4 *lb. blade bone of pork*
> 2 *large cooking apples*
> 2 *small leeks, cleaned and chopped*
> 4 *cloves*
> ½ *pint cider*
> *black pepper, salt*

Score pork rind with sharp knife. Place piece of foil on a roasting tray and place pork in the centre, rind side up. Clean and chop the leeks. Peel, core, quarter and slice the apples. Then lay them round the joint, along with the chopped leek. Pour in the cider, let the cloves float around in the liquid. Sprinkle black pepper over the pork. Now wrap foil loosely to cover pork and bake at Gas Mark 7, 450°F. for approximately 2¼ hours. Then open foil, sprinkle rind with salt and continue cooking uncovered for about 20 minutes. When you remove meat to serving dish place apple and leek round it and use the cidery juices as a gravy (thicken it if you like). Delicious.

Pork Loaf

Cut cold and serve with salad.

> ½ *lb. old white bread*
> 2 *lb. fairly lean raw pork*
> 1 *small onion, finely chopped*
> 2 *tsp. salt*
> 1 *tsp. white pepper, pinch sage*
> *milk or water*

Cut bread into cubes, and soak in milk or water. Mince pork coarsely (better still, *buy* it minced). Squeeze excess moisture from bread and add to meat, sage, onion and seasoning. Mix thoroughly, grease a 2 lb. loaf tin, and press mixture into it. Bake for 2–2½

81

hours, in a very moderate oven (Gas Mark 4, 350°F.). Turn onto plate, and allow to cool.

Pork and Potato Packs

A meal that cuts washing up, and cooks potatoes along with the meat.

> 1½ *lb. new potatoes*
> 6 *lean pork chops*
> 1½ *oz. butter*
> 6 *oz. sliced mushrooms mixed with* 1 *medium chopped onion*
> *lemon juice, salt and pepper*

Scrape potatoes, and slice very thinly; put in a pan of cold water, bring to the boil, continue cooking 1 minute, then drain. Meanwhile, cut six pieces of foil and rub them over lightly with butter (each foil piece should be big enough to wrap into a *loose* package). Arrange drained potato slices over butter, sprinkle with salt and pepper. Lay chops on potatoes, cover with mushroom and onion mixture, season well, add lemon juice and dot with butter. Wrap foil loosely into packs, pinching edges well together. Put on baking sheet, bake at Gas Mark 5, 375°F. for about 1–1¼ hours. Serve with juices poured round, and with a salad side plate.

Pork and Beans

Budget meal, with haricots and vegetables, eking out the meat.

> 1 *lb. haricot beans, soaked overnight*
> 2 *onions*
> 1 *leek*
> 2 *carrots*
> 1 *lb. cheap streaky pork*
> 1 *heaped tsp. paprika*
> *about* 2 *level tsp. salt (according to taste)*
> 1 *level tbsp. tomato purée*
> *chopped parsley (optional)*
> *oil, for frying*

Cook the haricot beans in the same water they've soaked in, very gently, until they are soft (about 2 hours). Dice onions, leek and carrot and fry all these in oil, then add to the beans. In the same oil fry the pork, diced, until crisp. Add pork to the beans and vegetable mixture, then stir in paprika, salt and tomato purée. Continue to cook slowly, till the meat is really tender – about ¾–1 hour. Add some chopped parsley at the end.

Beef and Pork Bake

A dish to feed eight large appetites.

> 1 *lb. lean minced beef*
> 1 *lb. minced pork*
> 2 *large onions, peeled and chopped*
> 1 *green pepper, seeded and chopped*
> ½ *lb. sliced mushrooms*
> 2 *cloves crushed garlic*
> *small can tomatoes, plus juice*
> 1 *tsp. Tabasco sauce*
> *salt and pepper*
> 12 *oz. noodles, uncooked*

Brown meats in a large pan. Add onion and green pepper, and cook a further 10 minutes. Add mushrooms, crushed garlic, tomatoes with juice, Tabasco sauce, salt and pepper. Stir in the uncooked noodles, and bring to the boil. Cover, and cook in the oven at Gas Mark 4, 350°F. for about 30–45 minutes. Garnish with chopped parsley.

Sweet and Savoury Pork Chops

> 6 *pork chops*
> 2 *tbsp. favourite packet stuffing (sage and onion best, I think)*
> 4 *tbsp. boiling water*
> 2 *dstsp. orange marmalade*
> 1 *chopped cooking apple*
> *salt and pepper*

Mix stuffing with boiling water, marmalade, apple and salt and pepper. Spread over chops, parcel in foil, and bake near oven-top for about 1 hour at Gas Mark 5, 375°F. Open foil for a further 4 or 5 minutes, to brown stuffing.

WAYS WITH LIVER

Lovely Liver

'Mm, lovely liver', says Caroline when I bring this dish to the table. And here's the way she likes it.

> 1½ *lb. liver, thinly sliced*
> 6 *rashers streaky bacon, rindless and chopped*
> 2 *medium onions*
> 15 *oz. can tomatoes*
> 1 *tbsp. tomato purée*
> *Worcester sauce, bay leaf, salt and black pepper*
> 1 *tbsp. flour*
> 1 *large apple, peeled, cored and chopped*

Sprinkle flour over liver. Melt butter in pan. Fry floured liver slices over gentle heat, about 4 minutes each side. Then fry the bacon. Fry peeled chopped onions, and then the apple. As each thing's done, put into a casserole dish. Finally put can of tomatoes, tomato purée and seasonings into casserole. Stir everything up together, put lid on, and cook in a fairly hot oven (Gas Mark 6, 400°F.) for 1 hour – or if you want to go out for the morning, cook it longer at a lower temperature.

Liver Parcels

Prepare the parcels early in the day, if you like, ready to put in the oven later on.

> 6 *slices of liver*
> 6 *rashers any sort bacon*
> 1 *medium onion, chopped*
> 2 *tsp. chopped parsley*

3 *rounded tbsp. soft breadcrumbs*
2 *oz. butter*
squeeze lemon juice
salt and pepper

Cut liver into fairly thin slices (about ¼ inch), better still, ask your butcher to do it for you. Cut the same number of pieces of grease-proof paper, large enough to wrap the slices, and brush with oil. Chop onion and bacon and mix with breadcrumbs and parsley. Make mixture into soft paste with lemon juice and butter, seasoned. Spread thin coating of paste onto each paper, top with liver slice, then more paste. Fold into parcels, twisting ends to seal. Steam over hot water for about 20 minutes or bake in a preheated, moderately hot oven (Gas Mark 6, 400°F.) till liver is tender. Unfold papers and slide contents onto hot plate. (Tip: plunge liver in boiling water before cooking, to tenderise it.)

Teuton Liver

6 *slices liver (about ½ inch thick)*
3 *large onions*
3 *apples*
butter or margarine for cooking

Slice onions into rings, and cook them slowly in butter until they're soft, but not brown. Remove from the pan and keep warm while the liver slices cook in the same pan, with more butter added if necessary. Cook the liver gently, and for not too long, so that it is still slightly pink inside. Meanwhile, in a separate pan, and with fresh butter, cook the apples (peeled, cored and sliced into rings) until they too are soft. Combine liver, apples and onions on a dish. Serve with a very soft purée of potatoes, and gravy made from the pan juices.

Liver Slices

For 16 slices.

1 *medium sized onion*
1 *oz. margarine*

¾ *lb. liver (try lamb's)*
2 *cups Basic Scone Mix made up as on p.* 202 *but minus sugar,
salt and pepper*
3 *eggs*
1 (5 *fl. oz.) carton yoghurt*
2 *tbsp. milk*
chopped parsley

Prepare a fairly hot oven (Gas Mark 6, 400°F.). Peel and finely chop onion. Melt margarine in a frying pan and fry onion until soft but not browned (about 5 minutes). Chop liver finely and add to onion. Cook for further 5 minutes. Make up scone mix, adding a little salt and pepper to dry mix first. Then turn on to floured board, knead lightly, roll out, and use to line a 10 inch by 6 inch shallow baking tin. Place eggs, yoghurt, milk and some salt and pepper in a basin, beat well together. Spread onion and liver mixture in lined tin and pour over egg mixture. Bake just above centre of oven for 10 minutes then reduce temperature to very moderate heat (Gas Mark 4, 350°F.) for a further 15 minutes. Sprinkle with chopped parsley, cut into 16 slices and serve warm, or cold with salad.

Pilaf

The East is responsible for plenty of cheap cooking ideas. Pilaf is one of them, and this version just one of dozens.

1 *lb. liver*
6 *rashers bacon*
1 *large onion, sliced in rings*
2 *cups chicken stock*
2 *cups rice*
margarine for frying
salt and pepper

Cook rice the casserole way (see p. 105) replacing water with chicken stock (home-made or from bouillon cubes). About 20 minutes before it's ready, cut liver in small cubes and fry gently in margarine till lightly browned. Season with salt and pepper. Fry the onion till tender and add this to liver and put in dish in oven. Crisp a few bacon rashers and add these. When the rice is cooked, toss liver mixture into it, and serve.

(*N.B.* Try this recipe also using cooked pieces of *pork* or *ham* instead of the liver.)

FISH FAVOURITES

All the recipes here use fresh fish, though frozen equivalents can be used for many of them. For recipes using tinned fish and seafoods, see the section headed **Store Cupboard Dishes.**

Cod and Bacon

A good meal that you can prepare in 15 minutes, start to finish.

> 6 *cod steaks or fillets*
> 2 *oz. butter or margarine*
> 6 *rashers bacon*
> 6 *tomatoes*
> *lemon juice, pepper*
> *To garnish : lemon and parsley*

Sprinkle cod with lemon juice and season with pepper. Melt butter and brush grid of grill pan with a little of it. Put fish on grill pan grid, brush with a little more butter, and grill under high heat 5 minutes. Turn, brush with remaining butter, top with bacon rashers and well seasoned tomato halves. Grill another 4 or 5 minutes. Garnish. If you're really in a panic, serve with instant mashed potatoes, and tinned green beans. If you've got time to prepare fresh vegetables, so much the better.

Kedgeree

With the rice cooked in advance, a kedgeree can be prepared in about 15 minutes. Incidentally, it's a good breakfast dish as well as a main meal. Here are two ways of cooking it.

Traditional Kedgeree

> 6 *cups cooked rice*
> 1½ *lb. smoked haddock, smoked cod, or kippers*
> 2 *hard-boiled eggs*
> 3 *tbsp. butter*
> *pinch of ground nutmeg*
> *salt and pepper*
> *juice of 1 lemon*
> *fried onions* (*optional*)

Pour boiling water over fish in a dish, and leave for a few minutes while you separate the whites and yolks of eggs and chop them finely. Flake the fish. Melt fat in large pan and add fish and rice. Cook gently till all is hot. Add seasonings, lemon juice and egg whites and heat again. Pile on hot dish and decorate with egg yolk. Garnish with parsley and wedges of lemon (with lots of fried onion too, if you like it).

Creamy Kedgeree

> 1½ *lb. haddock unsmoked* (*or other white fish, e.g. cod*)
> ¾ *pint milk*
> 9 *oz. cream cheese*
> *grated rind 1 lemon*
> 4 *cups cooked long grain rice*
> 1 *can sweet corn*
> *seasoning*

Put milk in pan, and add dash of salt and pepper to taste. Gently cook the haddock in this until tender. Then drain the fish (reserving the liquor) and flake the flesh. Cream the cheese till soft, work in the fish liquor, beat in fish flakes. Now add the lemon rind, sweet corn and rice, stirring well till all are blended. Check seasoning. Serve garnished with tomatoes and parsley, or with green pepper strips.

Smoked Haddie Roll

> 1½ *lb. smoked haddock*
> 3 *cups cooked rice*
> 5 *hard-boiled eggs, chopped*
> *chopped parsley, pepper and melted butter*
> *pastry (see Pastry Mix, p. 39)*

Roll out an oblong of pastry (made from 2 cups of your dry mix, or using a ready-to-roll pastry). Cover this completely with rice, then sprinkle on hard-boiled egg. Follow with chopped parsley, pepper and melted butter. Lay on fingers of uncooked smoked haddock. Roll, pinch edges together, and bake at Gas Mark 6, 400°F. till pastry is nicely golden. Cut in slices to serve.

Fish Salad Mayonnaise

Use fresh or tinned fish, and any assortment of the following: chopped onion, quartered tomatoes, cubes of cucumber, slivers of sweet red or green pepper, cooked haricot beans. Use in proportions to suit yourself, but there should be at least as much fish as salad, and preferably rather more. Blend well together with enough of your long-lasting mayonnaise (see p. 47) to make it taste good. Serve surrounded with a ring of cold or warm new potatoes, well sprinkled with parsley.

Baked Sprats

> 2 *lb. sprats*
> 1–2 *oz. fat or margarine*
> *seasoning*
> *lemon wedges*

Cut heads off sprats, clean, wash and dry them well. Brush a flat tin with half the melted fat, and put in the sprats. Season and top with rest of fat. Bake at the top of a hot oven (Gas Mark 7, 450°F.) for 8–10 minutes or till sprats are cooked and slightly crispy. Serve with lemon wedges.

Whitebait with Barbecue Sauce

> 1½ *lb. whitebait*
> *seasoned flour*
> *deep fat for frying*
> *cayenne pepper*
> 1 *can condensed tomato soup*
> 2 *tbsp. sweet pickle*
> 1 *tsp. brown sugar*
> 1 *tbsp. vinegar*
> 1 *tbsp. Worcester sauce*

Pick over the whitebait, then toss gently in seasoned flour. Heat fat and fry whitebait till crisp and cooked. Drain well and sprinkle with cayenne pepper. To make sauce, place tomato soup, sweet pickle, sugar, vinegar and Worcester sauce into a pan and heat gently. Pour sauce into bowl and use as a dip for the crisp whitebait.

Mackerel in Foil

> 6 *mackerel*
> *salt and pepper*
> 3 *firm tomatoes*
> 1 *lemon*
> *parsley*
> 2 *oz. butter*

Clean the fish and remove heads and tails. Season well with salt and pepper. Lay each fish on a piece of buttered kitchen foil. Cut the tomatoes and lemon into slices then arrange alternate slices on each fish. Place a good sprig of parsley on top and dot with butter. Fold the foil up and seal into neat parcels. Place on baking sheet and bake in a moderate oven (Gas Mark 4, 350°F.) for 25–30 minutes, until fish is thoroughly cooked. Serve mackerel in the foil, or transfer to a serving dish, together with the juices formed during cooking.

Summer Kippers

Quantities aren't important in this. It's all a matter of taste. So buy as many kipper fillets as will match hunger – I reckon two per person. Skin them, put them side by side in a flat dish, and pour enough boiling water over them to cover. After 5 minutes drain off water, cut the kippers into thin strips. Put them back into the same dish (or in a clean one if you must), cover with finely sliced onion rings and sprinkle over with French dressing (see p. 46). Cover, and put in refrigerator or cold place till ready to eat. Serve with potato salad or any other vegetable salad.

Fish Fillets Baked in Sauce

> 6 fillets of fish, uncooked
> large onion, grated
> 2 tbsp. each chopped celery, green pepper and mushroom
> 1 can tomato soup, pepped up with 1 tsp. sugar and 1 tsp. salt, and dash of pepper
> salt and pepper

Cut fillets of fish in half. Sprinkle them with salt and pepper, the grated onion, chopped celery and finely chopped green pepper, and mushroom. Pour over a can of the 'pepped up' tomato soup. Bake in moderately hot oven (Gas Mark 5, 375°F.) for 25–30 minutes.

Cod 'n Lemon Bakes

> 6 potatoes, cooked but firm
> 6 cod fillets or cutlets
> lemon
> salt, pepper, parsley butter

Cut 6 large squares foil and butter them. Slice potatoes and make a 'bed' of them on the centre of each foil piece. Place a cod fillet on each potato bed. Sprinkle with seasoning to taste and top with a slice of lemon followed by a sprinkling of parsley and a knob of butter. Wrap foil round fish, sealing edges. Put parcels onto baking tray, and bake just above centre of a moderately hot oven (Gas Mark 6, 400°F.) for 30 minutes.

Egg Crisp

> 6 *eggs*
> 1 *lb. cooked, flaked white fish*
> 1 *pint cheese sauce (see p. 46)*
> 3 *tbsp. browned breadcrumbs*

Heat fish through in half the sauce. Turn into flat, ovenproof dish. Place eggs in boiling water for 5 minutes. Remove to cold water for 8 minutes. Take off shells carefully, because eggs are soft. Lay them on top of fish, pour over remaining sauce, sprinkle with crumbs (optional). Brown under hot grill.

SAUSAGE MEALS

Sausage and Chicken Bake

> 1 *lb. pack frozen mixed vegetables*
> 8 *oz. Ritz Crackers (or similar)*
> 1 *lb. small skinless sausages*
> 2 *10-oz. cans chicken soup*

Cook mixed vegetables as directed on pack. Place crackers between 2 sheets of greaseproof paper and crush, using a rolling pin. Set oven at Gas Mark 4, 350°F. Place mixed vegetables, sausages and chicken soup in a bowl, and mix well. Place half the sausage mixture in a 1½ pint pie dish, cover with half the crushed crackers. Add the remaining sausage mixture and top with remaining crushed crackers. Place on baking sheet and bake in centre of oven for 30 minutes. Serve hot.

Sausage Bean Pot

For the day they bring home a few hungry 'extras'!

- 2 *lb. pork sausages*
- 2 *lb. peeled and sliced onions*
- 2 *level tsp. each of paprika and sugar*
- 2 *cloves of garlic, peeled and crushed*
- *large (2 lb. 3 oz.) can peeled tomatoes*
- 1 *pint water*
- 4 *cans haricot beans (or their equivalent in ones you've pre-cooked yourself)*
- ½ *lb. salami, chopped*
- *salt and pepper*
- *chopped parsley to garnish*
- *oil for frying*

Fry sausages until golden brown. Cut into thick slices, keep on one side. Add a little oil to the pan and sauté onions until golden brown. Stir in sweet paprika, sugar and crushed garlic cloves. Add peeled tomatoes and water. Add salt and pepper to taste. Bring to the boil and simmer for 25 minutes. Drain the haricot beans and stir into the tomato mixture, together with sliced sausage and chopped salami. Simmer gently for 15 minutes. Turn into a deep serving dish. Garnish with chopped parsley. Serves 10.

Super Supper

Quick supper dish with a subtle, fruity flavour. Serve with potatoes, peas or sprouts.

- 2 *lb. sausages*
- 1 *large onion, finely sliced*
- 1 *large red or green sweet pepper*
- 15 *oz. can tomatoes*
- 2 *oranges*
- 12 *stuffed olives (optional)*
- 3 *large slices bread, buttered*

Grill sausages for about 10 minutes. Remove from pan. Put a small knob of fat in the pan, if there is not sufficient from the sausages, and fry the sliced onion. Remove seeds from the pepper and cut into strips. Add to the onion. Drain juice off tomatoes, and chop. Peel the oranges and slice finely. Slice the stuffed olives. Stir tomatoes, oranges and olives into the onion and pepper mixture, and heat for five minutes. Arrange sausages in ovenproof dish and cover with the fried mixture. Cut slices of buttered bread into triangles and arrange, buttered side up, around the dish. Cook at the top of a fairly hot oven (Gas Mark 6, 400°F.) for about 20 minutes or until bread is golden brown.

Frankfurters

These continental sausages make a pleasant change to ordinary ones, served with mashed potatoes, on a bed of tinned sauerkraut, or with salad. Pour boiling water over them and leave to stand in a covered pan for 5 or 6 minutes. Then drain and serve them.

Sausage and Cheese Toad

> batter made using 8 heaped tbsp. Bulk Batter Mix (see p. 43) or using 8 heaped tbsp. flour blended with ½ tsp. salt, 2 eggs and 1 pint milk
> 3 oz. strong, grated Cheddar cheese
> 1½ lb. chipolata or skinless sausages

Make up the batter. Stir in grated cheese. Fry sausages till almost cooked and put in ovenproof dish. Pour batter over. Bake at Gas Mark 6, 400°F. for 30–35 minutes till crisp and golden.

Sausage Pizza

> make up suet pastry using 3 cups Basic Suet Mix (p. 40)
> 1 tsp. Marmite
> 1 medium (15 oz.) can tomatoes

small onion
8 slices Cheddar cheese
6 cooked sausages

Roll out pastry into a circle large enough to cover a 10 inch ovenproof plate or 10 inch flan tin. Spread the Marmite over the pastry, then drain the juice off the tomatoes, and spread them over the pastry, too. Cover with very thin slices of onion. Bake in hot oven (Gas Mark 7, 425°F.) for 25 minutes. Cut the sausage into slices and arrange these on top of the cooked pizza base, followed by the slices of cheese. Return to the oven and bake for a further 10–15 minutes.

STORE CUPBOARD RECIPES

A selection of recipes for which the principal ingredient (shown in bold type) *comes out of can or packet.*

Store Cupboard Stroganoff

12 oz. pork luncheon meat
1 large sliced onion
fat for frying
2 tsp. vinegar
¼ pint single cream
1 large can condensed mushroom soup
large packet of noodles
sliced beetroot (optional)
chopped parsley

Cube luncheon meat, and fry with sliced onion till both are cooked and browned. Stir vinegar into cream to sour it. Add half of this soured cream and the undiluted condensed soup, to meat. (Seasoning isn't necessary, as meat and soup are seasoned well.) Cook slowly, for 10 minutes. Cook noodles till tender in plenty of bubbling water; drain and add knob of butter. Spoon pork mixture into centre of noodles to serve. Pour over the remaining soured cream, and garnish with sliced beetroot.

Spaghetti with Ham and Cheese Sauce

> 10 *oz. Leicester or Cheddar cheese*
> 1 large (14 oz.) can chopped ham with pork
> 2 *oz. butter or margarine*
> 2 *heaped tbsp. plain flour*
> $1\frac{1}{2}$ *pints milk*
> *salt and pepper*
> 1 *lb. packet spaghetti, cooked as on p.* 107

Grate cheese. Cut chopped ham with pork into $\frac{1}{2}$ inch dice. Melt butter or margarine in a medium sized saucepan, stir flour into it, and cook gently for about 2 minutes stirring without browning. Gradually add milk and bring to boil, stirring continuously. Simmer for 2 minutes. Add cheese and diced meat. Taste and season the sauce with salt and pepper, before pouring it over the hot, cooked spaghetti.

Corned Beef Hash

I suppose every family has its favourite hash recipe. This is ours.

> 6 *large cooked potatoes*
> 12 oz. can corned beef
> 1 *cup of salami, cooked sausage, bacon etc. (chopped)*
> 2–3 *oz. margarine*
> 3 *medium onions, sliced*
> *garlic powder, salt and pepper*
> *juice of half a lemon*

Now – dice and roughly fry the potato in plenty of margarine. Fry the onion, add the chopped up corned beef and everything else, and stir it about. When it's piping hot and seasoned just right – serve.

Corned Beef and Tomato Roll

> 2 *cups Scone Mix plus milk, or milk and egg, to mix* (*p.* 42)
> 1 *medium size onion*
> 1 *oz. margarine*
> **12 oz. can corned beef**
> 10½ *oz. can condensed tomato soup*
> 1 *tsp. Worcester sauce*

Prepare fairly hot oven (Gas Mark 6, 400°F.). Peel and slice onion. Melt margarine and fry onion in this till golden brown, then leave to cool. Cut corned beef into small pieces. Add sufficient of the milk to scone mix, to make a soft but not sticky scone dough. Turn onto a floured board, knead lightly. Press out to fit a greased oblong tin. Brush edges with milk. Place corned beef down centre of dough and onions on top. Fold dough over filling. Seal edges and ends together firmly. Place on the greased tin, sealed side downwards. With a sharp knife make several slashes on top, about 1 inch apart. Mix tomato soup, Worcester sauce and half a can of water together. Pour around roll. Bake in centre of oven for 30 minutes. When golden cut into 6 slices, and serve hot with vegetables. Or bake without the sauce and take on a picnic to eat the same day.

Tuna Mornay

> 1 *lb. cooked potatoes*
> 1 *oz. margarine*
> 2 *tbsp. milk*
> *seasoning*
> **2 7-oz. cans tuna**
> 1 *pint cheese sauce* (see p. 46, or if you're really pushed, use packet sauce mix)
> *garnish : parsley and tomato*

Mash potato, beat in margarine, milk and seasoning. Line shallow, ovenproof dish with it, then put in flaked tuna. Make the cheese sauce; then spoon it over the fish. Bake in a moderate oven (Gas Mark 5, 375°F.) for 25–30 minutes, or till golden on top.

Note: Another tasty emergency tuna dish is to tip into a pan the contents of a packet of cheese sauce and a packet of parsley sauce. Make up with milk, as directed on packets. When the sauce is hot and ready, stir in the contents of 2 7-oz. cans of tuna. Add a dash of sherry, and a little chopped green pepper and grated onion. Serve straight from pan, or put into a low oven to keep hot till needed. With rice, this provides a good supper dish if friends arrive unexpectedly.

Sea Food Pilaf

> 2 *cups rice*
> 2 7-oz. cans tuna (*or crab or shrimps, or any mixture of these*)
> 2 *medium onions, chopped*
> 6 *large mushrooms, chopped*
> *any leftover peas*
> 4 *cups stock* (*chicken or made with chicken cube*)
> *seasoning*
> *oil for frying*

Heat oil to cover base of large-bottomed pan. Add the cups of rice and stir till all grains are coated. Pour in 4 cups boiling stock and bring all back to boil quickly. Cover and simmer on lowest heat for 20 minutes. Heat 4 tbsp. oil in a different pan and fry chopped onion in this till golden. Add cooked peas, chopped mushrooms and tuna, and season to taste. When hot, stir into the cooked, hot rice. Serve with lemon quarters and parsley sprigs.

Chinese Fish Balls

> 2 packets frozen cod fries
> *enough fat to cook them in*
> ½ *cup bottled sweet and sour sauce*
> 2 *tbsp. tomato purée*
> ½ *cup water*

Cook cod fries in hot fat, as per packet instructions. Blend together the sweet and sour sauce, tomato purée and water. Pour this sauce over the crisp cod fries and serve with boiled rice (see p. 103).

Pilchard Puff

> 1 lb. can pilchards in tomato sauce
> 1 *tsp. chopped onion*
> *pinch pepper*
> 8 *slices day-old bread*
> 3 *eggs*
> 2 *cups milk*
> *salt to taste*
> *butter*

Drain fish and reserve liquid. Flake fish, adding onion and pepper. Cut off bread crusts, butter them generously and cut diagonally in half. Arrange half the bread over base of greased baking dish. Arrange fish over these, then the rest of the bread. Beat eggs till light, then add milk, liquid from fish and a pinch of salt. Pour this over everything else. If you can leave it to stand for about half an hour, so much the better, otherwise, put it straight into moderate oven (Gas Mark 5, 375°F.) for 50 minutes–1 hour, till the puff is risen and golden.

Note: I've also made this with a fifty-fifty mixture of canned tuna fish and canned salmon.

Chilled Curried Chicken

> 2 large cans chicken curry
> 10 *oz. long-grained rice*
> *salt*
> 2 *lemons*
> 8 *oz. carton whipping cream*
> 2 *bananas*
> *a green salad to serve with it*

99

Chill the cans of chicken curry in the fridge for at least an hour. Boil the rice in plenty of salted water, and when it's cooked and drained, run cold water through it to separate the grains, then drain again. Grate the rind finely off one of the lemons and squeeze out the juice. Slice the bananas, pour the lemon juice over them, fork them lightly into the rice, and then spread this mixture over a dish. Open the cans of chilled chicken curry and empty the contents onto the rice. Whip the cream and spoon it down the centre. Sprinkle the grated lemon rind over the top and garnish with slices of the remaining lemon.

N.B. It's best to assemble this dish just before you want to eat it, though the rice can be cooked in advance.

MISCELLANEOUS

Cider Fondue

A protein-packed dish. Serve it with good portions of mixed salad, and it's a meal in itself.

> 1 *lb. grated Cheddar cheese*
> ¼ *pint dry cider*
> 2 *eggs*
> *salt and pepper*
> ¼ *tsp. Worcester sauce*

Melt cheese in the top of a double pan (or in a small pan standing in a larger one of boiling water). When melted, add the cider a little at a time, stirring. When this is hot but not boiling, stir in the beaten eggs. Season to taste, and add Worcester sauce. *Don't* allow to bubble. Serve in a hot dish, and hand out thick pieces of crusty French bread, or thick white or brown toast cut into cubes. Then let each child dip his own bread or toast into the fondue, and eat it coated with the cheesy goo!

Roman Savoury

> 1½ *cups fine semolina*
> 2 *pints hot milk*

4 egg yolks
plenty of strong grated cheese (about ½ lb.)
butter and margarine

Shower semolina into hot milk, stirring constantly until thickened. Beat in the egg yolks, about a quarter of the grated cheese, and a sprinkling of pepper and salt. Pat it out, to about ½ inch thick, on a buttered dish. Chill and then, when firm, cut into small rounds. Arrange these in a buttered dish and sprinkle each layer liberally with grated cheese. Dot with plenty of butter or margarine, and bake at Gas Mark 4, 350°F. till crisp and brown on top.

Fast Cheese Scallop

2 cups white sauce
1½ lb. cooked potatoes
dry mustard
salt and pepper
Worcester sauce
grated cheese to taste

Slice the potatoes and put them into a greased casserole dish. Make the white sauce (see p. 49) and season to taste with salt, pepper, mustard and Worcester sauce. Pour the sauce over potatoes, top with plenty of grated cheese and bake uncovered, at Gas Mark 4, 350°F. for 25 minutes.

Cheese Patties

12 heaped tbsp. flour
½ lb. cheese, grated
1 pint milk
2 eggs
4 level tsp. baking powder
1 level tsp. salt

Mix together all dry ingredients. Beat the eggs in with the milk. Then stir this liquid into the dry mixture. Spoon into well greased

patty tins and bake for 7–10 minutes in a fairly hot oven, Gas
Mark 6, 400°F. Serve with plenty of salad (new potatoes too, if you
like).

Cheese Pudding (good with sausages, chops, bacon)

> 9 *slices bread and butter*
> 3 *eggs*
> ¾ *pint milk*
> 4 *oz. grated cheese*
> 1 *good tsp. made mustard*
> *salt and pepper*

Take crusts off bread and butter slices, and cut 6 of them into little
squares. Put these in a buttered fireproof dish. Sprinkle cheese on
top. Beat eggs lightly and add to them the seasonings and mustard.
Blend the milk with the egg mixture and pour it all over the bread
and the cheese. Remove crusts from other 3 slices and cut each one
diagonally in half, so you get 6 triangles. Put these, buttered side
up, to make a roof. Cook in a moderate oven (Gas Mark 4, 350°F.)
till lightly set (25 to 30 minutes).

Savoury Pancakes

Pancakes, made and stored (see p. 143), can be the starting point of
a speedy main meal, allowing two or three per person depending
on appetite. Fill with minced ham and cooked chopped mushrooms
mixed with savoury white sauce; cheese sauce with shrimps; leftover
Kids' Curry (p. 66); cooked sausages mixed with a little chopped
fried onion and apple purée. Roll pancakes around filling, lay side
by side in greased fireproof dish, and mask with a white sauce, or a
cheese, tomato, or curry one, depending on the filling. Heat
through in moderate oven (Gas Mark 5, 375°F.) till sauce bubbles.

Trellis Flan

> 6 *standard eggs*
> 4 *rashers streaky bacon*

8 *tomatoes*
2 *cups mashed potato (fresh or packet)*
salt and pepper
caster sugar
1 *oz. butter or margarine*

Hard boil eggs for 10 minutes, crack, and leave in cold water to cool. Shell and dry on kitchen paper, then chop. Remove rind from bacon and cut it into long strips. Place tomatoes in a bowl and cover with boiling water. Leave for 1 minute, drain, then peel and chop (or just chop, if you've no time for peeling and don't mind the skin). Using a spoon, line a 10 inch flan tin (or pie plate) with potato. Arrange eggs in potato case, cover with chopped tomatoes, and sprinkle with some salt, pepper and sugar. Arrange bacon in a 'trellis' design on top. Dot with butter. Put in a hot oven (Gas Mark 7, 420°F.), near the top, and bake for about 25 minutes or until the bacon is crisp.

How to Cook Rice

Anyone who can cook rice successfully, with grains separate, and firm, yet tender, can knock up a string of meals in minutes. Because once cooked and drained, rice can be put into a covered container, and kept for 2 or 3 days in a refrigerator or cool place. Then it can be re-heated and topped with hard-boiled eggs, sliced and in cheese sauce: with Kids' Curry (p. 66) or other curries: or with any savoury sauce (Rice Bolognaise makes a change from Spaghetti Bolognaise). It can be mixed with cooked minced meat to stuff tomatoes, marrow, courgettes, or green peppers baked in the oven. It can blend with chopped crisp salad things and a good mayonnaise, as a summer dish.

If you're already a proficient rice chef, skip this. But if it comes out more like a damp pudding than a fluffy shower, here are some tips.

1. Choose the ordinary long grain rice (if you can get it, try Basmati rice, as a change).

2. Put on a really large pan filled with cold, salted water – the larger the pan, the more room the rice will have to move about, and the less likely it is to absorb all the water, and start to stick and burn.

3. Bring water to a fast boil, then tip in the rice. Stir it about, and stir a couple more times till water comes back to boil. This will stop the rice settling to the pan's bottom in heaps.

4. Cook for about 10 minutes, or until tender but firm. Depending on the rice, cooking times vary slightly. I start checking for texture (using a spoon to get out a few grains of rice) after about eight minutes.

5. When satisfied that it's as you want it, tip it all into a large colander, and wash through well with plenty of cold water. Leave to drain.

6. When you want to eat the rice spread it in a wide shallow dish, or on a large ovenproof serving dish, and cover with foil or with a cloth (the latter is better because it absorbs any moisture). Heat through in a preheated moderate oven (Gas Mark 4, 350°F.) for about half an hour, or until hot – the shallower the rice and the larger the dish, the quicker it will heat.

How to Cook Rice/2

That's the method I think most foolproof. But here's another which some cooks swear by.

Measure out 1 pint of water for each cup of rice. Put in $\frac{1}{2}$ level tsp. salt per pint of water. Bring it to the boil, and when it's boiling, put in the rice. When it's back to boil, put on the lid and in 10 to 15 minutes it will have absorbed the water and be cooked. What I don't like about this is, that if you have to answer the door bell, or wipe up the puppy's puddle, by the time you come back, the rice is sometimes starting to catch and burn.

If you get on with this method, however, you might try cooking your rice in a packet soup mix – made up the way the directions tell you. Or in tomato juice mixed with an equal quantity of water. If you're serving it with duck, cook it in orange juice mixed with just a little water. If the liquid evaporates before the rice is cooked, you can always add just a little more.

When I'm cooking rice, I allow two piled cups of rice for 6 of us, but get to know your own family's capacity and stick to it. Remembering that it's often useful to have some left over, because if you have to get mid-week meals for just one or two people, the rice can be heated through.

And now – after all this – some rice dishes.

Rice in Casserole

> 2 *cups long grain rice*
> 2 *cups water*
> 1 *tsp. salt*

Put the rice and salt in a casserole. Boil the water, and pour it over the rice. Cover the dish and cook in a moderate oven (Gas Mark 4, 350°F.) for about 40 minutes. Test by squeezing grains between thumb and finger; and if there's no hard core of uncooked starch, the rice is done. If necessary, allow remaining water to evaporate by removing the casserole lid for last few minutes. Fluff lightly with a fork, before serving.

Dressed-up Rice

A tasty way to use leftover rice – or cook rice specially for it if you like. Simply melt a good knob of butter (or margarine) in a heavy bottomed pan. When hot, dollop in the cooked rice, and cook over gentle heat, stirring every now and then. When all the rice is hot and buttery, stir in chopped pineapple and chopped salted almonds; *or* raisins and chopped walnuts; *or* chopped green pepper and onion; *or* celery and mushrooms; *or* plenty of fried onion and chopped hard-boiled egg.

Risotto

A pence-wise way to make a little meat stretch over several appetites.

> 6 *oz. streaky bacon*
> ½ *lb. leftover pork, ham or beef*, or 1 *can of salmon or tuna*
> 2 *onions*
> 4 *eggs*
> 2 *oz. margarine (or cooking oil)*
> 3 *cups long grain rice*
> 1 *rounded tbsp. chopped parsley*
> *salt and pepper*
> *finely grated cheese*
> 1½ *to* 1¾ *pints stock*
> ¼ *lb. mushrooms, chopped*

Finely chop onion, remove rind and bone from bacon and meat or fish being used, and cut into small pieces. Hard boil eggs for 10 minutes, cool and shell. Melt margarine in a saucepan and fry onion, bacon and mushrooms for 4 minutes. Stir in rice and cook for 2 minutes stirring until all the fat is absorbed. Add stock, stir well, cover and cook over lowest heat for 15 minutes. Remove lid, add chopped meat or fish, and cook for a further 5 minutes, stirring. Add extra stock if necessary. Chop hard-boiled eggs and carefully stir them into the rice (or decorate the top of the risotto with the eggs before serving). Stir in parsley and seasoning to taste. Place in a warmed serving dish and serve at once with a bowl of finely grated cheese.

Caper Rice

> 2 *cups long grain rice*
> 1 *pint white sauce (your own, or using packet mix)*
> 8–12 *frankfurters*
> 3 *tbsp. capers*
> 1 *oz. butter*
> 2 *eggs, hard boiled*
> *paprika*
> *salt and pepper*

Cook the rice and while it's cooking, make the white sauce. Cut the frankfurter sausages into chunks and add them and the capers to the hot, prepared sauce. Keep hot. When the rice is cooked, drain it, stir in the butter till it melts and press into a buttered ring mould – or just arrange it in a ring on serving dish. Pour the sausage and caper mixture into the centre of the rice ring. Decorate with slices of hard-boiled egg and paprika.

Walnut Rice

As an accompaniment for chops, boiled gammon etc. instead of potatoes.

> 3 *cups hot cooked rice*
> ½ *cup coarsely chopped walnuts*
> 6 *tbsp. butter*
> 2 *tbsp. Worcester sauce*

Melt butter and stir in the Worcester sauce. Add nuts, and brown them. Mix well together with the hot rice and keep in a covered dish in a low oven, till ready to serve.

Fried Rice and Shrimps

Melt 2 oz. butter in a pan. Add 4 cupsful cold boiled rice. Toss well, add a large can of shrimps or prawns, a few chopped up pieces of cooked ham or bacon, and 1 tbsp. finely chopped olives. Cook over gentle heat, stirring occasionally. When all is hot, blend in 1 tsp. soy sauce and a well beaten egg.

How to Cook Spaghetti
(also noodles, and other kinds of pasta)

The principle is the same as for rice, allowing as much water space as possible for the spaghetti to snake about in. As with rice, don't forget to salt the water, and also add just a dash of cooking or olive oil, or even a dab of margarine. Spaghetti sticks together, given the chance, but this will keep the strands nicely apart.

Cooked till 'al dente' (that's to say, tender yet 'bitey') pasta is at its best. Or do it a little longer, if you prefer. Cooking time is generally about 20 minutes, but I start checking after 15 minutes. An Italian girl I know tests spaghetti by throwing it against the tiled kitchen wall. If it drops to the floor, it's not ready; if it sticks, it's done. (Trouble with this is that it also sticks if it's horribly, hideously *over*-done. Still I pass the tip on for what it's worth.)

Once the spaghetti's cooked, it's best eaten as soon as possible. If it has to wait awhile, put it in a covered dish in a low oven. If you want to re-heat it, the best way is to heat up another big pan of water, till boiling, tip your already cooked spaghetti into it, for just long enough to heat through – about 2 minutes is usually enough time.

Once spaghetti's cooked, serve it with the bolognaise sauce on p. 109; with the ham and cheese sauce on p. 96; or with a quick sauce made by heating 1 large can tomatoes, dash Worcester sauce, fried chopped onion, and seasoning. Real addicts like it, too, with loads of grated cheese and butter. Or with melted butter blended with crushed garlic.

Incidentally, this same cooking method applies to noodles, macaroni and so on, though cooking times vary according to the thickness and type of pasta.

One Pot Spaghetti Cheese

> 1 *lb. packet spaghetti (allow extra if all appetites are very large)*
> 1 *tbsp. cooking oil*
> 6 *beaten eggs*
> 3 *oz. butter*
> 3 *tbsp. grated Parmesan (more if you like)*

Cook the spaghetti as on p. 107 but only leave it to boil for 1 minute. Then, remove pan from heat. Cover with a large enough folded teacloth, and press the lid down firmly over this. Leave the pan alone for 30 minutes. Strain off the water and stand the pan of spaghetti over tiniest heat possible. Then quickly mix into it the beaten eggs and Parmesan. Serve steaming hot.

Bolognaise Sauce to serve with spaghetti

1 *lb. minced beef*
1 *medium can tomatoes*
1 *large onion*
1 *or* 2 *tbsp. tomato purée mixed with* 1 *cup water*
basil
bay leaves (two or three)
salt and black pepper
1 *tsp. brown sugar*
1 *dstsp. vinegar*
fat for frying

Chop and fry the onion in a little cooking fat or oil. Add the meat and stir around with the onion for a few moments. Add everything else, stir, bring to a bubble and then lower heat to simmering point. Simmer for about 1–1½ hours with an occasional stir, checking seasoning before serving and adjusting it if necessary.

Gnocchi

A short cut to making those tiny light dumplings that are delicious either with bolognaise sauce (above) or with butter and grated cheese.

½ *lb. cream cheese*
2 *beaten eggs*
4 *tbsp. flour*
2 *tbsp. grated Parmesan cheese*

Mix everything, then shape into tiny balls and roll in a little flour. Drop into a pan of well-boiling salted water, and cook for about 4 minutes or until the gnocchi have risen to the surface of the water.

Cheese and Bacon Slices

The mustard gives this savoury a good flavour, but *doesn't* taste hot.

3 *cups Suet Mix, p.* 40 (*or* 1 *cup suet and* 2 *cups S.R. flour*)

pinch salt
water to mix
3 tsp. made mustard
6–8 rashers streaky bacon, de-rinded and chopped
4 oz. grated cheese

Blend the Suet Mix (or suet and flour) and salt, with enough water to make a pliable dough. Divide pastry into halves. Roll out one half, and line shallow baking tray (12 inch × 9 inch). Spread it with the made mustard, arrange bacon pieces over this, and sprinkle with grated cheese. Brush pastry edges with milk. Roll out remaining pastry and use to cover filling. Press pastry edges together, brush with milk and bake at Gas Mark 6, 400°F. for about 25 minutes. Cut into slices, and serve hot with vegetables or cold with salad.

Macaroni Cheese

There's nothing new about good old McCheese – but there are days when you don't have basic white sauce in store (p. 49) and even the fairly speedy business of cheese sauce making seems too much bother. And that's the time to try either of these quick 'n easy versions:

McCheese 1

For every 2 cups of uncooked macaroni you need:

2 cups of strong flavoured grated cheese
1 cup evaporated milk
salt and pepper
½ level tsp. dry mustard

Cook the macaroni (as for spaghetti on p. 107) unless it's quick macaroni in which case follow packet instructions. Roughly stir everything else in a pan, and heat *gently*, stirring occasionally. Soon it'll thicken and bubble. At this point, blend with the already cooked, drained pasta. Then eat it. If there's time for a finishing touch, put the McCheese in a dish at the top of a fairly hot oven to brown, or grill.

McCheese 2

For every 2 cups macaroni, you need:

> 4 tbsp. *instant, dried skim-milk powder*
> 1 tsp. *ready-made mustard*
> 1 heaped *cup crumbled mature flavour cheese*
> *a little extra cheese for topping*
> *seasoning to taste*

Cook macaroni in plenty of boiling salted water, till tender but still firm. Strain off the water but leave a couple of tablespoons of it behind. Put the pan over low heat, then add to the hot but not boiling water the instant dried milk powder, and made mustard. When that's blended, add the cheese. Season to taste and stir heartily. Stir macaroni and sauce together in a greased dish, crumble more cheese over the top, dot with butter flakes, and brown under a hot grill. Serve instantly.

And to end this section a few etceteras.

Subtle Sauce

> 3 oz. *cream cheese*
> 2 tbsp. *milk*

Beat the cream cheese a little. Add the milk gradually, beating until smooth. Heat gently. Use as coating sauce over cod or salmon cutlets, garnished with parsley and lemon. Or serve on hot vegetables

Simple Sauce Tartare

> ¼ *pint of mayonnaise (bought, or as on p. 47)*
> 2 tbsp. *tarragon vinegar (or water, if lemon juice was used in making mayonnaise)*
> *finely chopped mixed pickles and chopped parsley to taste*

Put mayonnaise and vinegar (or water) into a heatproof basin standing in a pan of boiling water. Stir in pickle and parsley. When hot, serve with any boiled, grilled or fried fish, with hot or cold seafood.

Five-minute Pickle

> I *small can peeled tomatoes (minus liquid)*
> I *cup finely chopped cucumber*
> I *tsp. sugar*
> I *tbsp. chopped spring onions*
> $\frac{1}{8}$ *cup vinegar*
> I *tsp. ginger*
> I *tsp. salt and pinch pepper*

Mush up the tomatoes, then blend in everything else.

Instant Tomato Ketchup uncooked

> I *small can peeled tomatoes (minus liquid)*
> I *tbsp. sugar (or less, if preferred)*
> I *tsp. salt, pepper*
> $\frac{1}{4}$ *cup vinegar*
> I *tsp. made mustard*
> *pinch cloves and ground nutmeg*

Mash tomatoes and stir in other ingredients (if you have a liquidiser, just whizz everything round in that).

Quick Chutney

> I *cup thick jam (e.g. plum)*
> $\frac{1}{8}$ *cup vinegar*

1 *tsp. curry powder*
1 *tsp. ginger*

Blend all together.

VEGETABLES
as accompaniments and as main dishes

Sweet Corn with Ham

If they like sweet corn, a large cob with a slice of ham each is a meal in itself.

Here's one easy way to cook the corn cobs.

After you've removed the husks and silk from them leave them to stand in salted water from 20 minutes–1 hour. Drain well, brush with soft butter and sprinkle with salt and pepper. Wrap individually in double thickness foil, twist the ends to seal, and cook in a pre-heated hot oven (Gas Mark 8, 450°F.) for 20–30 minutes. (If you know the family will be rolling in at different times to eat, try the method on p. 178.)

Sweetcorn Rounds

Delicious with ham and fried chicken.

    1 *large can sweetcorn kernels*
    1 *large finely chopped onion*
    4 *heaped tbsp. S.R. flour*
    4 *tbsp. chutney*
    4 *eggs, lightly beaten*
    salt and pepper
    fat for deep frying

Dump the drained sweetcorn, onions, flour, chutney, eggs and seasonings together, and stir till blended. Heat the fat, and fry rounds of the mixture till crisp. Drain well on kitchen paper and serve at once.

Corny Tomato Casserole

At least, it's corny to us now because we've had it so often. To you,
it just might be new.

> 5 *slices day-old bread, cut in small cubes*
> 2 *oz. melted butter*
> 6 *large, ripe, firm tomatoes*
> 11 *oz. can whole kernel corn*
> 1 *medium onion, chopped*
> ½ *level tsp. salt, good sprinkle pepper*
> 3 *beaten eggs*

Toss half the bread cubes in melted butter and place the other half
in the bottom of a buttered ovenproof dish. Top with layers of
tomato slices, then with corn kernels mixed with onion and seasoning. Pour over the eggs. Sprinkle the buttered bread cubes on top.
Bake in a moderate oven (Gas Mark 5, 375°F.) for 35–40 minutes
till hot and golden brown.

Make Ahead Tomato Salad

Make this a few hours in advance so that the flavours have time to
mature.

Put a layer of sliced, unpeeled tomatoes in a shallow, medium-
size bowl. Top with a layer of sliced spring onions. Sprinkle with
seasoning, salt and pepper, whatever fresh herbs are available and
French dressing (see p. 46). Repeat layers.

Tomato Crumble

> 2 *onions, finely chopped*
> 2 *oz. margarine*
> 2 *cups grated Cheddar cheese (strong)*
> 1⅔ *cups day-old breadcrumbs*
> 1 *lb. tomatoes, peeled and sliced*
> *salt and pepper to taste*

2 eggs
8 tbsp. milk and water, or stock

Add onion to melted margarine in small saucepan. Fry over low heat until golden brown. Remove from heat and stir in cheese and breadcrumbs. Brush a medium-sized pie dish with melted margarine, then put in a thin layer of the cheese and breadcrumb mixture. Add layer of tomato slices. Sprinkle with salt and pepper. Continue these layers, ending with one of cheese and breadcrumbs. Beat the eggs, add the milk and water, or stock, and pour this over the mixture. Bake near the top of a fairly hot oven, Gas Mark 7, 425°F. about 20 minutes until golden brown, lightly set and heated through.

Nut and Tomato Mince

Tasty on its own, or with chicken, ham or chops.

2 onions, finely chopped
4 oz. butter
3 cups finely chopped mixed nuts
1 lb. tomatoes
3 rounded cups soft breadcrumbs
2 tsp. Marmite
1 tbsp. chopped parsley
salt, pepper and nutmeg

Melt butter in pan, add onion, and cook till tender. Add chopped nuts, and skinned and sliced tomatoes to mixture. Then add everything else, and stir thoroughly to blend. Cover pan and leave on gentle heat for about 5 minutes, or till mixture is piping hot. Serve on hot plates, sprinkled with nutmeg and accompanied by a side salad.

Oven-baked Tomatoes

When tomatoes are inexpensive, they make a good vegetable, cooked in the oven along with baked chops, or a liver dish. Here are two ways:

1. Without foil

> 12 *tomatoes*
> 4 *oz. margarine*

Make a tiny slit at the top of each tomato, and place in a greased heatproof dish. Dot with knobs of margarine. Bake near the top of a preheated, moderate oven (Gas Mark 4, 350°F.) for 25–30 minutes.

2. With foil

Cut required number of tomatoes in half, and place on a large piece of foil. Sprinkle with salt, pepper and a little vinegar and sugar. Top with flakes of butter or margarine. Wrap and seal edges. Bake near the centre of a fairly hot oven (Gas Mark 6, 400°F.) for 30 minutes.

Celery au Gratin

A vegetarian main dish.

> 2 *cans of celery hearts, drained (or braise fresh celery, as below,*
> *till tender and use that)*
> 4 *rashers of streaky bacon, chopped*
> 1 *pint cheese sauce (see p. 46, or use packet mix)*
> *salt and pepper*
> 4 *oz. grated cheese*

Cut the celery into pieces and arrange in dish. Fry the bacon until crisp, crumble it, and sprinkle over the celery. Make up the cheese sauce, seasoning it and adding most of the cheese. Pour the sauce over the celery, sprinkle with the remaining cheese, and cook under a medium grill until golden-brown.

Braised Celery

> 1 *large, or 2 small heads celery*
> *water, sugar and butter or margarine*

Discard leaves and base of the celery. Wash and cut into 2 inch pieces, then place these on a large piece of foil. Sprinkle with a tablespoon of water and a little sugar and salt and pepper. Dot liberally with butter or margarine. Fold foil over and press edges together. Cook on the middle shelf of a moderate oven (Gas Mark 4, 350°F.) for 1–1½ hours.

Carrots and Celery

To serve with a main dish.

> 6 *carrots*
> 4 *large sticks celery*
> *pinch sugar*
> 1 *tbsp. chopped parsley*
> 2 *tbsp. butter or margarine*

Prepare and slice vegetables. Cook together in boiling salted water till they're tender (about 20 minutes). Drain. Add sugar, parsley and margarine to them, toss well and serve.

Buttered Carrots and Potatoes

A vegetable dish to slow cook all day.

> 1½ *lb. carrots*
> 2 *lb. potatoes*
> 2 *oz. butter*
> 1 *tsp. salt*
> 1 *tsp. brown sugar*
> 2 *tbsp. top of the milk*
> 1 *tbsp. chopped parsley*

Peel the carrots and potatoes and slice into rings. Melt the butter in a pan, add the carrots and potatoes, put on pan lid, and cook over low heat for about 5 minutes giving the occasional stir. Add all seasoning, sugar and top of milk. Leave to simmer lightly for a couple of minutes then put into a tight-lidded greased oven dish. Put straight away at the bottom of the same oven in which you're slow cooking a roast (see p. 62) and leave for the same amount of time. When ready to serve, sprinkle with the chopped parsley.

Chinese Celery

Cut a head of cleaned celery into strips. Place in saucepan, sprinkle with salt, and barely cover with cold water. Bring to boil gently. Allow to boil for 1 minute then drain immediately. While still hot, toss in a dressing made of 2 tbsp. vinegar, 2 tbsp. olive oil, and 2 tbsp. soy sauce.

Stir-fried Vegetables

Excellent with fish dishes.

> 2 *onions*
> 1 *green pepper*
> 4 *sticks celery*
> 1 *oz. butter*
> 1 *tbsp. oil*
> *salt and pepper*
> 9½ *oz. can beanshoots*

Gently fry sliced onions, pepper and celery in butter and oil for 5 minutes stirring occasionally. Season. Add drained beanshoots. Cook for 5 more minutes.

Bacon and Beans

> 2 *big onions*
> 2 *cans broad beans (or equivalent fresh and precooked)*
> 3 *rashers bacon, cut into pieces*

Chop onions and mix with cooked broad beans. Put in casserole dish with bacon pieces on top, and heat at Gas Mark 4, 350°F. till the bacon is crisp.

May's Marrow

(Equally good using leeks, cucumbers, or as a variant of cauliflower cheese.)

Peel marrow, slice it and de-seed. Cook it your favourite way – I do mine in about ½ inch water very slowly. When *just* tender (usually about 10–15 minutes after coming to boil) drain. Place in a casserole, top with halved, hard-boiled egg, and cover with a well-flavoured cheese sauce. Brown quickly under the grill, or at the top of a hot oven.

Leek and Tomato Salad

> 6 *young leeks*
> 6 *skinned tomatoes*
> 1 *lettuce*
> *clove garlic*
> 1 *tsp. dried basil,* 1 *tsp. dried chervil* (*optional*)
> 3–4 *tbsp. French dressing*

Put herbs to marinate in the dressing for ½ hour. Wash leeks and slice white part finely (keep outside greener parts to use for a casserole or soup). Cut skinned tomatoes into eights. Wash and dry the lettuce, then break up roughly into manageable pieces. Rub inside of a salad bowl with a cut clove of garlic and arrange lettuce at the base. Arrange leeks and tomatoes on the lettuce, and sprinkle with the herbs in French dressing.

Oven Mushrooms

Brush a sheet of cooking foil with oil or melted butter. Place mushrooms on the sheet, in a single layer, sprinkle with salt and pepper, cover with foil and seal. Bake in a moderate oven, Gas Mark 5, 375°F. for about 15 minutes.

Peas with Bacon

Try them with a casseroled chicken dish.

Remove rind and bone from 6 rashers streaky bacon and cut into strips. Fry in a saucepan until browned. Place with 1½ lb. frozen peas (just thawed) in a small casserole. Sprinkle with salt and pepper and add ¼ pint boiling water. Cover and cook on lower shelf of hottish oven for 1 hour. Drain. Add knob of butter and serve.

Monaco Onions

A vegetable accompaniment for cold meats.

> 1 *lb. small peeled shallots, equal size*
> 1½ *cups water*
> ½ *cup vinegar*
> 1 *tbsp. olive oil*
> 3 *tbsp. caster sugar*
> 2 *tbsp. tomato purée*
> *a little chopped celery*
> *salt and pepper to taste*

Combine all ingredients in a saucepan and bring to the boil. Lower heat and simmer for 1 hour. Chill before serving.

Nutty Cabbage

> 1 *large white cabbage*
> 1 *large chopped onion*
> 1 *cup chopped nuts*
> 3 *oz. butter*
> 1 *oz. dark brown sugar*
> 1 *cup stock*
> *salt and black pepper*
> 3 *tbsp. flour*
> 2 *cups hot milk*

Clean and shred cabbage coarsely, plunge into boiling water, strain and plunge into cold. Drain again. Melt 2 oz. of the butter and brown the onion in it, then add sugar and chopped nuts. Add stock, bring to boil then add cabbage and simmer till tender, with lid on. Make sauce by blending remaining butter with flour over gentle heat (or use prepared roux mentioned on p. 48). Gradually add hot milk, stirring, and continue to stir with wooden spoon till creamy and bubbling. Season with salt and black pepper. Then pour the sauce over the cooked cabbage and nut mixture before serving.

Potatoes

If the family love mashed potato, try it this way. Add grated cheese and a couple of egg yolks to mashed potatoes. Put in heaped table-spoons onto a greased tray. Bake till crisp in a hot oven (Gas Mark 7, 450°F.). *Or* add 2 egg yolks to the mashed potato then fold in 2 stiff egg whites. Put into a buttered dish, and bake in a moderate oven (Gas Mark 5, 375°F.) till puffy and golden.

Mushroom Spuds

Grate 6 medium potatoes (using grater with large holes), and put them in an ovenproof dish. Mix in can of condensed cream of mushroom soup, and half can of milk. Heat this, and pour over potatoes. Bake, uncovered, at Gas Mark 4, 350°F. for 1¼ hours.

Jacket Potatoes

Choose 6 large, even-sized potatoes, scrub and dry them, then prick them and brush with melted fat or cooking oil. Bake in the oven *either* for about 1½ hours (Gas Mark 3, 330°F.) or for about 45 minutes–1 hour in a fairly hot oven (Gas Mark 7, 425°F.). Serve with butter, and pepper and salt. Good with a blob of cream cheese, too.

Bombay Chestnuts

A main dish that's quick and easy if the chestnuts have been roasted and peeled in advance. Fewer people these days have open fires for roasting, but the chestnuts can be cooked in a baking tin in a hot oven. Pierce skins first. Timing depends on their size.

> 1¼ *lb. chestnuts, roasted and peeled*
> 1½ *oz. sultanas and currants, mixed*
> 1 *carrot*
> 1 *medium Spanish onion*
> 2 *very large cups vegetable water*
> 2 *tbsp. butter*
> 2 *tbsp. vinegar*
> 2 *tbsp. mango chutney*
> 2 *tsp. curry powder*
> 1 *tbsp. flour*
> *plain boiled rice*

Peel and chop onion and carrot, and brown in butter. Add flour to pan, with curry powder, and cook 2 minutes. Gradually add vegetable water, stirring. Heat to boiling, reduce heat and add everything else. Simmer 25 minutes and serve on plain hot rice.

Homecoming Soup

So called because you set your oven to its lowest setting, put in the soup, and it's ready 7–8 hours later.

> 1 *cup split peas, washed and drained*
> 3 *small carrots, cubed*
> 2 *large onions, grated*
> 4 *bay leaves*
> 1 *tsp. salt and a little pepper*
> 1 *tsp. Worcester sauce*
> 3 *pints stock, or* 1½ *pints water and* 1½ *pints milk*
> 4 *rashers lean bacon, chopped*

Put everything, willy-nilly, into a saucepan. Bring to the boil, then pour straight into a large lidded oven dish (or make a cover with foil). Put the dish in the centre of an oven on its lowest setting. Leave for 7–8 hours.

Vegetable Risotto

A cheap main dish. Pieces of fried bacon can be added if you like.

2 *onions*
2 *carrots*
4 *sticks celery*
2 *large tomatoes*
4 *oz. margarine*
3 *cups rice*
2 *tsp. Marmite*
1 *pint stock or water*
juice of 1 *lemon*
1 *tbsp. finely chopped parsley*
salt and pepper
4 *heaped tbsp. finely grated cheese*

Peel the onions and carrots, and cut them into small cubes. Scrub celery and cut that into small pieces. Peel and chop tomato. Melt margarine in saucepan, and add the prepared vegetables. Toss over a gentle heat for 3–4 minutes. Wash rice, drain it, then add it to the vegetables. Cook over gentle heat, stirring occasionally until rice looks transparent. Dissolve Marmite in stock or water, and add with lemon juice to pan. Cover pan and cook gently for about 30 minutes, or until the liquid has been absorbed and the grains of rice are tender but still whole. (Stir occasionally, and if necessary add a little extra liquid.) Just before serving, stir in finely chopped parsley, and add salt and pepper according to taste. Serve with finely grated cheese.

CHAPTER FIVE

Puddings and Other Afters

QUICK AND EASY

A selection of puds that are either fast to prepare just before the meal, *or* that you can prepare ahead of time ready for instant serving.

Danish Slices

> 1 *piled cup cream cheese*
> 1 *cup chopped eating apples*
> 1 *cup chopped walnuts*
> ½ *cup chopped dates*
> *top of milk*
> 6 *slices rye bread*

Cream the cream cheese with the top of the milk till really soft. Add everything else, and spread onto slices of rye bread.

Date and Apple Puffs

> 2 *large cooking apples*
> 4 *oz. stoned dates*
> 4 *heaped tbsp. S.R. flour*
> 2 *standard eggs, beaten*
> 2 *level tbsp. caster sugar*
> 4 *oz. margarine*

Peel apple and coarsely grate into a large bowl. Finely chop dates and add to bowl. Stir in flour, egg and sugar, and mix well. Melt margarine in a large frying pan, then fry dessertspoonfuls of the mixture over moderate heat for about 5 minutes turning once. Drain on kitchen paper and keep warm. Pile onto a warmed serving dish. Serve with apricot jam, sauce or custard.

West Indian Wrap-ups

Cut 6 squares of foil. On each piece place a peeled banana with some tinned pineapple pieces, lemon juice, a little brown sugar. Wrap the foil into little parcels, twisting ends to secure, and cook in moderate oven (Gas Mark 6, 400°F.) for about 20 minutes.

Banana and Chocolate Cream

> 6 *bananas*
> 3 *tbsp. caster sugar*
> ¾ *cup double cream*
> *vanilla essence*
> 3 *oz. chocolate vermicelli or grated chocolate*
> *glacé cherries*

Skin bananas and mash. Add sugar and vanilla essence to taste, and then the cream. Put mixture in individual dishes. Cover top of mixture with chocolate and a cherry. Serve when cold.

Banana Crunch

> 15 *oz. can ready made custard (or make the custard using* 1 *heaped tbsp. custard powder,* ¾ *pint milk and* 1 *level tbsp. sugar)*
> 4 *large bananas*
> 8 *level tbsp. flour*
> *mixed spice*
> 2 *oz. butter or margarine*

2 *level tbsp. caster sugar*
2 *level tbsp. oats*

Butter a dish and pour the custard into it. Slice in the bananas, and stir to mix. Put the flour in a bowl with spice and rub the fat into this. Then add sugar and oats and toss the mixture together. Sprinkle it over the bananas and custard, and bake in the middle of a moderately hot oven (Gas Mark 5, 375°F.) for about 40 minutes or till the crumble is pale golden.

Three-Fruit Cocktail

6 *bananas*
1 *lb. can grapefruit segments*
2 *oranges*
optional maraschino or glacé cherries

Peel and slice bananas, drain grapefruit (reserving juice), and add fruit to bananas. Squeeze oranges and pour juice over grapefruit and bananas, adding enough grapefruit juice just to cover. Chill. Garnish with cherries.

Blackberry Shortcake

2 *cups plain flour*
4 *tsp. baking powder*
4 *level tbsp. sugar*
2½ *oz. margarine*
pinch salt
milk
1½ *lb. blackberries mashed with sugar*
whipped cream or mock cream (p. 44)

Mix flour, baking powder, sugar, margarine and pinch of salt with enough milk to make a soft dough. Divide into two flat cakes, brush one with margarine, place the other on top of it and bake at Gas Mark 6, 400°F. for 25 minutes, or till cakes are golden and cooked in the centre. When cooked, separate cakes, spread lower one with half the blackberry and sugar mash, and mock cream. Replace upper cake, pile with remaining blackberries mashed with sugar. Serve warm with cream or mock cream.

Blackcurrant Dessert

> 15 oz. *can blackcurrants*
> 2–3 *tbsp. sugar*
> 3 *tbsp. cornflour*
> *water*

Make the blackcurrant juice up to 1 pint with water, and boil it with the sugar. Mix the cornflour with a little more cold water, and when the syrup boils, stir this in. When smooth and thickened, add the fruit and carry on till it's all simmered for three minutes. Pile into individual glasses, and chill.

Blackcurrant Fluff

Take one of the cans of boiled, chilled evaporated milk that you've got in the fridge. (You haven't? See p. 44.)

To either a whole small can or half a large one, allow one 14 oz. (or thereabouts) can of blackcurrant pie filling. Whip the evaporated milk for a few moments, till it comes up thick and frothy. Then gently fold in the can of pie filling till it's well blended and takes on a mousse-like consistency. Pour into 6 small individual glasses.

You can do this with *any* flavour canned pie filling, and get a whole range of desserts. Change its character too, by sprinkling with meringue pieces, chopped nuts etc.

Cherry Delight

This looks impressive when your children bring other children in for tea, but couldn't be simpler.

Quantities don't matter too much.

Put meringues (bought or home made) in a dish. Heap on vanilla ice cream and follow this with whipped cream (or packet mock cream). Meanwhile, heat a can of cherries in their syrup (Morello are best, but it doesn't matter) and pour these over at the last moment before serving.

This is good for adult entertaining, too, specially if the cherry syrup is spiked with rum, brandy or a favourite liqueur!

Orange Cheese Rolls

12 oz. cottage cheese
1 rounded cup seedless raisins, chopped
6 oz. icing sugar, sieved
grated rind and juice 2 oranges
orange wedges and icing sugar for serving
plus pancakes, made using recipe on p. 143 or p. 144

Mix together cottage cheese, raisins, icing sugar, orange rind and juice. Divide mixture between 12 pancakes, roll, place on a lightly greased tin and heat through for 30 minutes at Gas Mark 5, 375°F. Serve dusted with icing sugar, and with orange wedges.

Hot Orange Peaches

1 large can peach slices
2 heaped tbsp. orange marmalade
whipped cream or evaporated milk

Strain the juice off the peach slices. Put the slices in a serving dish. Heat juice with the orange marmalade. Pour over peach slices and serve with whipped cream or evaporated milk.

Honey-Bake Pears

12 canned pear halves
¾ cup honey
¼ cup lemon juice (or a little more depending on taste)
1½ tsp. cinnamon
3 tbsp. butter

Put pears in shallow buttered dish, pour over lemon juice and honey. Sprinkle with cinnamon and dot with butter. Bake at Gas Mark 4, 350°F. till hot – about 25 minutes.

Grecian Pears

> 1 *small can dessert pears*
> *cottage cheese*
> *slivered almonds*
> 2 *tbsp. chocolate powder*
> 1 *dstsp. sugar*
> 2 *tbsp. top of the milk*

Fill pear centres with cottage cheese, sprinkle with almond slivers and refrigerate. Heat together the top of the milk, chocolate powder and sugar, and pour this hot sauce over the cold pears when serving.

Panned Pineapple

> 6 *oz. margarine*
> 4 *rounded tbsp. soft brown sugar*
> 1 *can pineapple titbits*
> 6 *level tbsp. caster sugar*
> 2 *large beaten eggs*
> 4 *heaped tbsp. S.R. flour*
> *pinch salt*

Mix half the margarine and all the brown sugar in a frying pan. Melt but don't boil. Put drained pineapple in frying pan. Cream remaining margarine with caster sugar till smooth, stir in the beaten eggs and then the flour and salt. Spread over pineapple rings, cover pan, and cook on lowest heat for 30 minutes. Serve with cream.

Rhubarb Meringue

A useful pud, because half of it can be made in advance, while the last touches of baking can be quickly and easily done.

2 *lb. rhubarb*
granulated sugar or honey to taste
1 *dstsp. water*
2 *cups desiccated coconut*
4 *oz. seedless raisins*
3 *egg whites* ⎫
6 *tbsp. caster sugar* ⎭ *topping*

Cook the rhubarb gently with the granulated sugar or honey and water, in lidded pan, till done. Blend with 1½ cups of the desiccated coconut, and the seedless raisins, and put into pie dish. Whisk egg whites till very stiff, then gradually whisk in caster sugar and remainder desiccated coconut. Pile on top of rhubarb, and bake for about 30 minutes in centre of a very moderate oven (Gas Mark 3, 325°F.).

Skillet Strawberries

An unusual hot strawberry dish, given to me by an American friend. Worth trying if you can get the fruit cheaply.

4 *oz. butter*
2 *cups white crustless bread, diced*
½ *cup brown sugar*
1 *tsp. cinnamon*
1 *lb. strawberries*

Melt butter in frying pan, add the tinily diced bread, and cook gently, stirring till cubes are golden. Add brown sugar and cinnamon; cook and stir till bread is crisp. Add hulled strawberries and cook gently, stirring constantly, for another couple of minutes. Serve hot, topped with spoons of cold ice cream.

Summer Special

½ *lb. cream cheese*
3 *tbsp. icing sugar*
1 *tbsp. lemon juice*

pinch nutmeg
1 pint strawberries, sliced
whole strawberries to garnish

Beat cheese, sugar, lemon juice and nutmeg together till fluffy. Starting with layer of sliced strawberries put alternate layers of strawberries and cream cheese mixture into 6 small glasses. Top each with a whole berry. Chill well.

Fruit Salad with Citrus Dressing

Prepare and dice any fruit, for a fruit salad. Then drizzle all over with honey thinned with lime juice, or mayonnaise thinned with fresh orange juice.

Crunchy Topped Stewed Fruit

    1 cup crushed sweet biscuits
    1 cup cornflakes
    1 tbsp. brown sugar
    2 tbsp. melted butter or margarine
    2 tbsp. coconut
    2 tbsp. chopped walnuts
    ½ cup sultanas
    (Last two can be omitted)

Mix everything together, and sprinkle over any purée of stewed fruits, or canned pie filling. Bake about 25 minutes (Gas Mark 5, 375°F.) to brown.

Butter Pudding

Serve with canned or stewed fruits – or make double quantity and eat as a pudding in its own right with custard or sweet white sauce.

    9 heaped tbsp. plain flour
    pinch salt
    6 oz. unsalted butter

14 *tbsp. caster sugar*
1 *egg*
brown sugar, cinnamon

Beat egg and divide into two bowls. Beat together the butter and caster sugar. Combine one half of the egg with the butter and sugar and then work in the flour. Butter a small square baking tin, and press out dough to cover tin. Brush top of cake with rest of egg and sprinkle with brown sugar and cinnamon. Put in fairly hot oven (Gas Mark 5, 375°F.) for about 20 minutes or till the outside is golden, but the inside still a little soft. Mark into squares or triangles while warm. Take out when cake has cooled.

Fruit Foursome

A very different kind of hot pudding.

4 *oz. oats*
4 *oz. stoned dates*
4 *oz. raisins*
4 *oz. chopped hazelnuts*
4 *tbsp. condensed milk*
4 *oz. demerara sugar*
4 *oz. margarine*
cream to serve

Grease the tin and line with a round of greased paper. Chop dates and raisins, mix with nuts and oats. Melt margarine and condensed milk and sugar in a pan. Pour this over the oats mixture; blend. Turn into tin and press well to the sides. Bake at Gas Mark 4, 350°F. for about 40 minutes. Serve with cream, or eat as it is.

Raisin and Chocolate Bake

6 *heaped tbsp. plain flour*
2 *level tbsp. cocoa powder*
large pinch salt
4 *level tsp. baking powder*

3 cups soft white breadcrumbs
6 level tbsp. caster sugar
1 cup seedless raisins
½ lb. melted margarine
4 beaten eggs
few drops vanilla essence

Stir together flour, cocoa, baking powder, and salt. Stir in bread-crumbs, caster sugar, seedless raisins. Then mix in melted fat, eggs and essence. Stir thoroughly, tip into a 2 lb. loaf tin and cook 1–1¼ hours, or till cooked through in moderate oven (Gas Mark 5, 375°F.).

Honey Bake

4 level cups flour
8 oz. clear honey
3 oz. melted margarine
½ tsp. baking powder
½ gill milk
cinnamon, nutmeg

Put flour into a mixing bowl, pour in honey and melted margarine. Stir well. Dissolve baking powder in milk. Add to pudding mixture, flavour with pinch of cinnamon and ground nutmeg. Pour mixture into greased pie dish and bake in moderate oven for 1 hour. Serve with custard or apple sauce.

Fruit Cake Pudding

2 cups crumbled stale fruit cake
1 egg
1 tbsp. sugar
1 tsp. vanilla
½ pint milk
sherry and chopped nuts (optional)

Put crumbled fruit cake in ovenware dish, and sprinkle with a little sherry if you have some – add chopped nuts if liked. In a basin, beat up the egg with 1 tbsp. sugar, 1 tsp. vanilla and ½ pint milk. Pour all over the crumbled cake. Bake in slow oven (Gas Mark 2, 300°F.) for about 30 minutes.

Cream Crunch

> 1 *block vanilla ice cream*
> *a few brandy snaps*

Crush snaps into small pieces with rolling pin. Spoon ice cream into a dish and sprinkle the brandy snaps over it.

Strawberries and Yoghurt

> ½ *lb. strawberries*
> 3 *cartons natural yoghurt*
> 2 *tbsp. vanilla sugar*

Chop strawberries and blend with sugar and yoghurt.

Family Syllabub

A dessert to be drunk, rather than eaten. Make it quickly and serve straight away.

> ½ *pint Cydrax*
> 2 *eggs*
> 4 *level tbsp. caster sugar*
> *nutmeg*
> *sponge fingers*

Whisk all the ingredients, except the sponge fingers, together over a low heat until thick and frothy. Pour into individual glasses and serve immediately with the sponge fingers. Serves 4 to 6.

Meringue Creams

Crumble one merginue per person. (Buy meringues or see recipe on p. 219.) Fold into sweetened whipped double cream (or use

cheaper whipping cream). Add a few drops of favourite flavouring
– e.g. vanilla, rum etc.

Peach and Mincemeat Charlotte

> 8 oz. fresh white breadcrumbs
> 1 cup shredded suet
> 8 tbsp. demerara sugar
> ½ tsp. ground nutmeg
> 15½ oz. can sliced peaches, drained
> 5 heaped tbsp. mincemeat

Mix suet, breadcrumbs, sugar and nutmeg. Place layer of this
charlotte mixture on the base of greased ovenproof dish. Arrange
peaches on top, and cover with another layer of charlotte mixture.
Spread mincemeat over this and top with remaining charlotte
mixture. Press down with back of spoon and bake at Gas Mark 6,
400°F. for 30 minutes. Serve hot.

Sticky Pudding

> 4 thick slices white bread
> ¼ lb. butter
> 1 cup sugar
> ½ lb. golden syrup, scooped straight from tin is easiest (or 8
>   tbsp.)
> 1 cup milk (fresh or made with ½ cup evaporated and ½ cup
>   water)

Trim crusts off bread, cut into quarters, and soak in the milk for a
few minutes. Meanwhile, put the butter, syrup and sugar into a
heavy bottomed pan over medium heat. Stir till boiling and bubbling.
Put bread (carefully removed from the milk which it should just
have soaked up) into caramel mixture and bubble gently till golden.
Gently turn pieces over in the mixture if necessary. After 2 or 3
minutes transfer the golden, sticky bread pieces to a dish in a
moderately hot oven. Bring remaining sauce back to a brisk boil

till it's good and thick. Pour over the bread and leave in the oven, at the top, for about 15 minutes. Or if you're ready to eat straight away, put it under the grill to brown and crisp the top – the kids call this 'sweet crackling'.

N.B. A *very* sweet pud this, and strictly not for folks with tooth trouble.

Sweet Toasted Sandwiches

Make sweet sandwiches in the usual way – try a filling of lemon curd and sliced banana, or chopped nuts and apple purée. Cut off the crusts, then butter the top and bottom outsides of the sandwich, toast on both sides till crisp and golden. Time-saving tip is to prepare sandwiches in advance, wrap in aluminium foil, then toast when ready to eat.

Butterscotch Toasties

> 6 *slices bread*
> 2 *oz. butter*
> 3 *level tbsp. soft brown sugar*
> ½ *tsp. cinnamon*
> 4–6 *bananas, depending on size*

Toast bread, cream butter with soft brown sugar and cinnamon. Spread toast slices with cinnamon mixture, and cover with slices of banana. Heat under grill till sizzling.

Brown Bread and Butter Pudding

> 1 *granary or fruit malt loaf*
> 5 *oz. butter*
> 1¼ *cups sultanas*
> 4 *level tbsp. demerara sugar*
> 2 *eggs*
> 1 *pint milk*
> 4 *level tbsp. caster sugar*
> 1 *drop of vanilla essence*

Spread a little butter round a pie dish (about 2½ pint size) then butter the slices of granary bread, fairly thickly, cutting each slice in half diagonally. Mix the sultanas and demerara sugar and layer them into the dish with the bread and butter, keeping enough fruit and sugar to sprinkle over the top. Beat the eggs; then add the milk, caster sugar and vanilla. Pour this over the pudding, and sprinkle the remaining fruit and sugar over the top. Bake the pudding in a moderate oven (Gas Mark 4, 350°F.) for about half an hour then reduce the heat to Gas Mark 3, 325°F. for a further 10 minutes.

Yoghurt Fluff with Raspberries

> 2 egg whites
> 2 egg yolks
> ⅓ cup sugar
> ½ tsp. vanilla
> 3 6-oz. cartons yoghurt (or make your own, see pp. 156, 157)
> 1½ lb. washed, prepared raspberries

Beat egg whites to soft peaks. Beat egg yolks, sugar and vanilla until thick and lemon coloured. Fold egg yolk mixture into yoghurt. Fold in egg whites. Spoon about ½ cup of mixture over each serving of raspberries.

Yoghurt with Fruit

> 1½ lb. berries, juice of 1 small lemon (or 2 tbsp. bottled or canned juice)
> 2 cartons plain yoghurt
> sugar to taste

Wash fresh berries and drain them thoroughly (or, if using frozen berries, defrost them). Gently combine all ingredients, sweetening to taste. Serve in a bowl or little dishes.

Bananas with Yoghurt

> 6 *bananas*
> ½ *cup peeled, blanched almonds*
> 2 *tbsp. soft brown sugar*
> 2 *cartons unflavoured yoghurt*

Mash bananas, chop almonds, and stir together with the sugar. Mix in the yoghurt and serve.

Jiffy Sweets

Top plain biscuits with an egg white whipped with 2 heaped tbsp. caster sugar, and sprinkled with finely chopped walnuts.

Mash canned raspberries, add whipped cream and sugar to taste. Chill well.

Blend 1 tbsp. cottage cheese with 1 chopped apple (per portion).

Serve a mixture of dried fruits (apples, pears, peaches etc.) ... a bowl of raisins and shelled nuts ... a packet of figs or dates.

Give them uncooked porridge oats, mixed with any chopped unsalted nuts, sultanas, and a few bits of fresh fruit, to which they add milk or cream, and maybe sugar according to taste. (A kind of breakfast Muesli, but why confine a good idea to one particular meal?)

Put out a bowl of fresh fruit. Give them crisp apples with hunks of crumbly Lancashire or Cheshire cheese.

Apple In-and-out

A quick and nice version of old-fashioned apple pud.

> 3 *cups Suet Mix, p.* 40 (*or* 2 *sups S.R. flour and* 1 *cup suet and pinch salt*)
> 6 *level tbsp. sugar*
> 2 *large cooking apples*
> *milk*

Peel, core and chop apples small. Mix Suet Mix (or flour, suet and salt) with sugar and chopped apples, then blend to a fairly stiff consistency with milk. Bake for 1 hour at Gas Mark 5, 375°F. Turn out of dish, sprinkle with sugar and serve with Devonshire cream.

Tangy Treacle Tart

> 3 cups Suet Mix, p. 40 (or 1 cup shredded suet and 2 cups S.R. flour)
> 1 tsp. ground cinnamon
> milk to mix
> 6 tbsp. golden syrup
> grated rind and juice of 1 lemon
> 1 cup fresh white breadcrumbs

Blend suet mix, or suet and flour, with cinnamon and enough milk or water to make firm pastry dough. Roll out pastry, and line a 10 inch greased flan tin. Blend all remaining ingredients to make the filling. Pour this into pastry case, sprinkle with extra breadcrumbs if you like, and bake 30 minutes in a fairly hot oven (Gas Mark 6, 400°F.). Serve hot.

Fruity Poly

> 3 cups Basic Suet Mix, p. 40 (or 1 cup suet blended with 2 cups S.R. flour)
> 14 oz. can fruit pie filling
> 1 tbsp. granulated sugar
> milk

Make suet pastry, stirring the Basic Suet Mix (or suet and flour) with enough milk to make a soft yet not sticky dough. Roll suet pastry into oblong. Spread pie filling over pastry to within 1 inch of edges. Brush pastry edges with milk, and roll up loosely. Seal join firmly. Pinch ends together and crimp. Place, join side down, on baking tray. Brush with milk, sprinkle with sugar and bake in a fairly hot oven (Gas Mark 6, 400°F.) for 25–30 minutes.

Cherry Dumplings

>2 cups Suet Mix, p. 40 (or 3 heaped tbsp. suet and 6 heaped tbsp.
>   S.R. flour)
>3 tbsp. caster sugar
>3 tbsp. desiccated coconut
>12 glacé cherries, chopped small
>1½ pints milk

Mix together the suet mix (or suet and flour), sugar, coconut and cherries, with enough of the milk to make a firm dough. Shape into 12 dumplings. Bring remaining milk to below boiling, then simmer the dumplings in this till they're cooked – about 8–10 minutes. Serve hot, with the milk liquor poured over. If you prefer, use the milk to make custard.

Alternative to the cherries is to use 1 tbsp. sultanas and 1 tbsp. currants.

Apricot Dumplings

>16 oz. can apricots
>2½ cups Suet Mix (p. 40)
>water to mix (about 6–7 tbsp.)

Drain apricot syrup into large saucepan, and heat. Meanwhile blend suet mix with enough water to make soft but not sticky dough. Break off small pieces of the dough, roll into balls with your hands, and drop into the syrup once it starts boiling. Cover pan and simmer 10 minutes. Add apricots. Simmer another 5 minutes and serve immediately.

Apple Cheese Crumble

>1 lb. cooking apples
>½ cup grated cheese
>3 heaped tbsp. plain flour
>4 tbsp. butter
>(or use 5 rounded tbsp. Pastry Mix (p. 39) to replace flour and
>   butter)

½ *tsp. cinnamon*
6 *tbsp. brown sugar*
pinch grated nutmeg

Peel and slice apples, and mix with grated cheese in baking dish. Soften butter and mix into flour, as for pastry (unless using dry Pastry Mix in which case this is already done). Blend in all other dry ingredients. Sprinkle over apples and cheese, and bake 40–50 minutes at Gas Mark 5, 375°F. till fruit is tender. Serve hot.

Pear and Apricot Crumble

CRUMBLE
> 1 *cup plain flour*
> 4 *oz. butter*
> (*or use* 5 *tbsp. dry Pastry Mix (p.* 40) *in place of the flour and butter*)
> 8 *level tbsp. caster sugar*
> *grated rind of* 1 *lemon*

FILLING
> 3 *Conference pears, peeled, cored and sliced*
> 15 *oz. can apricots, drained and roughly chopped* (*reserve syrup*)
> 1 *tbsp. lemon juice*

Crumble: Sift flour and caster sugar into a bowl. Mix in lemon rind and rub in butter until mixture resembles fine breadcrumbs. (If using Pastry Mix, blend it with sugar, then mix in lemon rind.)

Filling: Arrange pears and apricots in a 2½ pint ovenproof dish. Mix together apricot syrup and lemon juice and pour this over the fruit. Sprinkle crumble over fruit. Bake in a hot oven (Gas Mark 7, 425°F.) for 25–30 minutes until golden brown.

Sweet Fillings for Pastry Cases

You can use all kinds of things to fill ready prepared flan cases (made using one of the recipes on p. 39 or on pp. 230–5). For instance, stewed fruit, canned pie fillings, packet desserts and whips, instant whip blended with fruit purées. And here are four more ideas.

Egg and Lemon Filling

> 5 rounded tbsp. Bake Mix (p. 41)
> 1 egg
> rind of 1 lemon grated
> 1 tbsp. caster sugar
> juice of 2 lemons

Put Bake Mix in a basin. Beat the egg and gradually add this and the lemon juice to the Bake Mix, little at a time. Fold in lemon rind blended with the sugar. Bake in a 10 inch pastry case for 20–25 minutes (Gas Mark 3, 325°F.). The filling should have become a curd, and started to brown.

Hazelnut and Lemon Filling

As above but add chopped hazelnuts to taste.

Coffee Almond Filling

As above, but replace lemon juice and rind with 1 tbsp. strong black coffee, and add some flaked blanched almonds.

Apple and Coconut Filling

To each 3 tbsp. apple purée (canned or home made) blend in 2 tbsp. strawberry jam, and 2 tbsp. coconut.

Pancakes

Before plunging into a few recipes, remember that pancakes can be eaten straight away, *or* they can be stored and successfully re-heated.

To store them either wrap them well in foil or polythene, tying the bag end or sealing the foil (when they will last well for 3 or 4 days). Or refrigerate them, separated by sheets of waxed paper, in an airtight container. Or freeze them, by interleaving them with oiled greaseproof paper or polythene, wrapping in heavy duty foil from which all air's been expelled before sealing; they last for about 2 months, and thaw out fairly quickly for use if unwrapped and spread out at room temperature for about 15 minutes.

How to re-heat the pancakes? Roll them round a filling – or roll, moisten with a thin syrup and dot with butter – then put in a buttered ovenproof dish, cover and re-heat in a moderate oven (Gas Mark 5, 375°F.) for 30 minutes. Alternatively, fry them individually, for about ½ minute each side.

'Filling' ideas are to spread them with cream cheese mixed with chopped nuts, then serve with a jam sauce: to add 2 level tbsp. melted orange marmalade to the batter mixture: or to fill with any sweetened fresh or canned fruit purée.

Another idea. As the pancake cooks, cut it into pieces with a couple of knives or forks, and to these shredded cooked pieces add a sprinkling of sultanas and a good knob of butter. (A specially good idea if it's an off-day and the pancakes *will* keep breaking or losing shape!)

Pancakes Using Bulk Batter Mix

These good old children's favourites are speediest of all to prepare if you use your Bulk Batter Mix (see p. 43).

> 9 *tbsp. Bulk Batter Mix*
> 1 *small egg beaten into enough milk to make ⅔ cup of liquid*
> 4 *tbsp. warm water*
> *butter for frying*

Put the mix into a basin, then gradually beat in the egg and milk mixture. Gradually beat in the warm water, and continue beating till everything's well blended. For each pancake, melt a knob of butter in the pan, and when this is hot and sizzling, pour in the batter – enough to cover the pan bottom thinly. When the underside is done (and as a rule this is when the top of the pancake begins to bubble) turn and cook the other side for about the same length of time.

Pancakes Starting from scratch

There'll be times when you run out of your Bulk Batter Mix. Or maybe you've decided that you're just not organised enough to keep and use the bulk mixes anyway. Well, here's how to make pancakes from scratch.

> 8 oz. *plain flour*
> ½ tsp. *salt*
> 2 *eggs*
> 1 *pint milk*

Sieve together flour and salt. Make a 'well' in the centre, and break the eggs into this. Stir, little by little drawing in flour from round the side. Gradually add enough milk to incorporate all the flour and make a thick paste. Beat very well to remove all lumps and give a smooth batter. Stir in remaining milk, little at a time, then beat or whisk thoroughly till small air bubbles appear over the surface. Cook pancakes as in previous recipe. You can use this batter straight away or let it stand a little.

As a rough guide, this recipe will make about 12 pancakes in a 5 inch pan, 10 pancakes in a 6 inch pan, and 8 pancakes in a 7 inch pan. Serve with traditional lemon juice and caster sugar, or with butter and sugar.

Batter Pudding Using Bulk Batter Mix

> 1 pint batter (*made using Bulk Batter Mix with 1 egg and* ⅔ *cup milk, or milk and water, blended as described above*)
> 2 oz. *cooking fat*

Put fat into baking tin and place a third of the way down the oven (Gas Mark 7, 425°F.). Heat till fat is at hazing point. Pour in batter, and bake for 25–35 minutes or till the pudding is well risen, golden, and firmish to touch. Serve with syrup, jam, or butter and sugar handed separately. If liked, a little caster sugar can be added to basic mix.

Note : milk alone gives a heavier batter, the milk and water mixture a lighter one.

Rich Batter Pudding

Made as for ordinary Batter Pudding, but use an extra egg in place of 1 tbsp. of the liquid.

Fruit Batter Pudding

> 1 *pint batter, made using Bulk Batter Mix* (*p.* 43)
> 2 *oz. fat*
> *fruit chopped into bite size pieces*

Follow method as in Batter Pudding (p. 144) but having filled pie dish to about ⅔ full, drop in fruit pieces to taste and bake about 30 minutes or a little longer at Gas Mark 7, 425°F. till nicely browned. Good with custard. (Raisin Batter Pudding is made by putting 6 oz. large washed and well-dried raisins into the hot fat *before* pouring on the batter mixture.)

Sweet Fritters

> 1 *cup Bulk Batter Mix* (*p.* 43)
> 1 *egg plus enough liquid* (*milk, water, sweet cider, fruit juice, syrup or fruit squash*) *to make* ¾ *of a cup*

Put the dry mix in a basin, and slowly add the egg and liquid, beating it in till everything's well blended. Beat for a further minute, then dip fruit to be coated into the mixure. Bananas, apple, pears, pineapple are specially good, and canned fruits as well as fresh can be used, provided they are *very* well drained first and blotted free of their juice (you can use juice from the can to make the batter if you like). Fry the fritters in a pan of deep hot fat (when they won't need turning) or in shallow, hot fat (when they will). When brown and crisp, drain on absorbent paper. If you make too much fritter mixture it will keep several days in the fridge in a covered container. If needed, add a little extra liquid, or give a good beat.

Sweet Fritters Starting from scratch

4 heaped tbsp. plain flour
1 egg beaten into ¼ pint milk
¼ tsp. salt

Make and use as in previous recipe.

Apple Pancakes

Unconventional pancakes, really quick to mix and prepare because the fruit purée is incorporated in the batter itself.

1 lb. apple purée (a can, or your own make)
4 heaped tbsp. plain flour
1 egg

Beat altogether in a basin, quickly, to a semi-thick consistency. Drop in large spoonfuls on a greased griddle or frying pan, and cook gently on both sides, like drop scones. Serve sprinkled with caster sugar, or with refrigerator cream (p. 44).

Quick Honey Cream Sauce to serve with any pudding

Put ½ cup honey in warm basin or stand basin containing honey in warm water for few minutes. Stir in ½ tsp. cinnamon, 2 or 3 tsp. lemon juice, ½ tsp. vanilla and ½–¾ cup cream or evaporated milk. Heat gently, but serve before boiling.

Instant Lemon Sauce

4 tbsp. sweetened condensed milk
grated rind and juice of 1 lemon

4 *tbsp. water*
vanilla essence to taste

Mix the condensed milk with the lemon rind and juice. Add the water, and a drop or two of vanilla essence. Serve cold on a cold or hot pudding.

Caramel Sauce for ice cream

½ *lb. caramels*
¼ *pint milk*

Place caramels in a small pan with milk, and heat slowly till the caramels have melted. Stir well, then pour into a serving jug for instant use.

Coffee Fudge Sauce

10 *heaped tbsp. soft brown sugar*
2 *oz. butter or margarine*
2 *tbsp. Camp coffee essence*
pinch ground ginger
4 *tbsp. evaporated milk*

Combine all ingredients, except evaporated milk, in a pan. Bring to the boil, stirring, until sugar dissolves. Allow to simmer gently for 1 minute. Remove from heat and stir in evaporated milk. Serve hot over ice cream or chocolate pudding.

Chocolate Fudge Sauce

1 *cup milk*
1 *tbsp. butter*
2 *cups sugar*
2 *tbsp. cocoa powder*
vanilla essence

Heat milk almost to boiling, add butter, sugar, cocoa, stir. Simmer all together till butter's melted, then remove from heat and stir in a few drops vanilla essence. If you want to do this in advance, put into a wide mouthed vacuum flask where it will keep well.

Cream Cheese Dessert Sauce

3 oz. cream cheese
3 tbsp. milk
sugar to taste

Beat together till smooth. Or add 3 tbsp. fruit juice instead of milk and sugar and beat till smooth. Serve with fruit in season, or canned fruit.

Syrup Sauce

As above, but with 1 tbsp. golden syrup replacing 1 of milk. Serve hot or cold with steamed pud.

Quick Chocolate Sauce 1

3 oz. drinking chocolate powder
2 tbsp. water
1 tsp. vanilla
top of milk or evaporated milk

Mix the chocolate and water in a small pan and bring to boil, stirring all the time. Add vanilla and dilute to desired thickness with milk or cream. Serve hot or cold.

Quick Chocolate Sauce 2

1 tbsp. cocoa
1 tbsp. butter
1 tbsp. golden syrup

Melt over gentle heat, boil for a few moments, stirring, and then serve hot over ice cream.

Quick Fruit Sauce using liquidiser

Put any stewed fruit, sweetened, into the liquidiser and blend till smooth. If necessary add a little water, lemon, orange or other juice to dilute to desired consistency. You can do the same thing with canned fruit, using whatever syrup is necessary for the right consistency.

Ice Cream Topping

Put 3 chocolate peppermint creams per person on a baking tray or fireproof plate in a low oven. When soft and melted pour this delicious, streaky hot sauce over cold ice cream. Lovely.

PLANNED IN ADVANCE

Lemon Ice-box Pie

SPICED CRUMB CASE
>3 oz. margarine
>6 oz. wholemeal biscuit crumbs
>10 rounded tbsp. soft brown sugar
>1 level tsp. each ground cinnamon, ginger and nutmeg

FILLING
>1 large can (15 oz.) evaporated milk, boiled and chilled (see p. 44)
>2 eggs, standard (separated)
>4 rounded tbsp. caster sugar
>grated rind and juice of 2 large lemons
>lemon jelly slices to decorate (optional)

To make spiced crumb case: Melt margarine and combine with

remaining crumb-case ingredients. Press into oblong tin (10 inch by 6 inch). Chill until set.

To make filling: Mix egg yolks with sugar, lemon rind, and juice, until thoroughly blended. Whisk egg whites until stiff, and evaporated milk until *very* thick. Fold both these into lemon mixture. Pour over prepared crumb case. Chill until set. Decorate with lemon jelly slices and serve cold.
N.B. At a pinch you can make this using unboiled evaporated milk, chilled for at least 2 hours.

Easter Cake

A version of the pashka eaten in Russia at Easter time and with no cooking involved.

> 1 cup each of:
> *cream cheese*
> *sour cream*
> *chopped mixed candied peel*
> *sultanas and currants mixed*
> *caster sugar*
> *softened, unsalted margarine or butter*
> *chopped mixed nuts*
> *plus 2 tbsp. chopped dates*

Mix well together and press into cold, rinsed and still damp flat tin, so that pashka is about 1 inch thick. Place in fridge overnight and serve with plain biscuits.

Christmas Pudding Dessert

If hot Christmas pudding after a hot Christmas dinner seems too much, try this alternative. It has the right, spicy festive flavour but is refreshing at the same time. You can make it a couple of days before you want to eat it.

> *4 oz. fresh white breadcrumbs*
> *¾ cup ground almonds*

2 *medium sized apples, minced*
2 *large carrots, finely grated*
2 *cups raisins (seedless)*
1 *cup sultanas or currants, or mixed*
¼ *cup glacé cherries*
4 *pieces preserved ginger (optional)*
3 *tbsp. mixed candied peel*
3 *tbsp. orange juice*
2 *or* 3 *tsp. grated orange rind*
touch of cinnamon
butter as needed to grease basin
custard or whipped cream

Mince together dried fruit, cherries and ginger and mix with minced apple. Add carrots, orange juice and rind, almonds and bread-crumbs. Flavour with cinnamon, according to taste. Put mixture into buttered pudding basin and press down firmly. Keep in fridge with weight on top; to serve, turn it out, and hand round custard or whipped cream.

Flask Fruits

This is a pud that cooks itself. All you do is warm a vacuum flask by letting some hot water stand in it for a few minutes. Empty this away, put as many dried fruits as your kids can eat at the bottom of the flask (remember that they'll swell) and fill up with boiling water. Leave for at least 2–3 hours. When you're ready to eat, so are the hot plumped-up fruits.

Spicy Topped Cream

¾ *pint milk*
1 (10 *oz. can) 'top of the milk' cream*
1 *packet vanilla flavour Instant Whip*
2 *rounded tbsp. caster sugar*
½ *to* 1 *level tsp. ground cinnamon*

Place milk and 3 rounded tbsp. of cream in a basin, add Instant Whip powder, and whisk until dissolved and thickened. Pour immediately into a 1 pint shallow ovenproof dish. Spread remaining 'top of the milk' over pudding. Chill for at least 1 hour. Prepare a very hot grill. Mix sugar and cinnamon together and sprinkle over pudding. Place pudding under grill, just long enough for the sugar to dissolve, and the top to crisp and brown lightly. Leave to cool. Serve pudding cold the day it is made.

Overnight Fruit Pudding

Can be mainly mixed the night before cooking.

> 1 *rounded tbsp. butter*
> $\frac{1}{2}$ *cup sugar*
> $\frac{3}{4}$ *cup boiling water*
> 1 *level tsp. bicarbonate of soda*
> 1 *cup mixed fruits (or sultanas)*
> 1 *tbsp. chopped peel*
> 1$\frac{1}{2}$ *cups plain flour (all white or half white, half wholemeal)*
> $\frac{1}{2}$ *tsp. salt*
> 2 *tsp. baking powder*
> 1 *beaten egg*
> $\frac{1}{2}$ *tsp. vanilla essence*

Place butter in pudding basin. Pour in boiling water. Add sugar and bicarbonate of soda. Stir till butter melts and soda dissolves. Add mixed fruits or sultanas, and chopped peel. Sift in flour and salt, and mix well. Leave to stand for several hours or overnight. In the morning, stir in baking powder, beaten egg and vanilla essence. Mix, cover with greaseproof and string, and put basin to steam in boiling water for 2$\frac{1}{2}$–2$\frac{3}{4}$ hours.

Spicy Bread Pudding

> 12 *oz. white bread*
> 2 *standard eggs*
> 4 *oz. margarine or butter*

4 level tbsp. caster sugar
1 level tsp. mixed spice
4 rounded tbsp. thick cut marmalade
about 2 cups dried mixed fruit (any mixture of sultanas, raisins, currants)
granulated sugar (for sprinkling – optional)

Grease a 10 inch × 6 inch oblong baking tin. Put bread, roughly torn up, into a bowl, and cover with boiling water. Leave 5 minutes. Squeeze till nearly dry, then beat till smooth. Beat egg, cut margarine or butter into small pieces and add to the bowl with sugar, mixed spice, marmalade, dried fruit and egg. Mix well. Pour into tin on level surface. Bake on lower shelf of moderate oven (Gas Mark 4, 350°F.) for 1½ hours, till firm and golden brown. Sprinkle with sugar if desired, and serve hot with custard. Good cold, too, cut into slices.

Cup Pudding

Providing you think about it in advance, this pudding is child's play to make because measuring and mixing are so simple.

1 cup each of:
flour
suet
soft white breadcrumbs
brown sugar
mixed dry fruit
milk in which 1 tsp. bicarbonate of soda is dissolved

Beat together thoroughly for a few minutes (or let a mixer do it for you), put into a greased basin, cover with greaseproof paper and steam for 3 hours. Serve with a sweet sauce or melted honey.

Boys' Pudding

1 lb. mincemeat
1 egg
3 oz. S.R. flour

Put mincemeat in basin. Beat in egg. Fold in flour. Put in greased pudding basin and cover with aluminium foil or pudding cloth. Steam for 1½ to 2 hours. Turn out and serve with custard.

Raisin Rice Pudding

1 *lb. can rice pudding* (*or same amount of home-made*)
⅓ *cup raisins*
2 *tbsp. double cream*
½ *tsp. vanilla essence*
4 *level tbsp. fine brown sugar*

Mix rice pudding, raisins, cream and vanilla essence, and put in ovenproof dish. Sprinkle sugar over top of pudding and put under grill till it melts. Cool and chill. If left for some time, the sugar blends in with the rest, and gives a good caramel colour and flavour.

Cold Honey Cream

6 *tbsp. honey*
¼ *pint double cream, whipped thick*
4 *eggs, separated*

Separate egg whites and yolks. Whip egg whites till they stand up in peaks. Beat egg yolks with honey, heat in the top of a double boiler till thick (don't let it boil). Leave to cool, then fold in egg whites and whipped cream. Chill in refrigerator.

Custards

Can be made in advance and stored in refrigerator for 2 or 3 days.

6 *eggs*
2 *tbsp. sugar*
pinch salt
2 *pints milk*

Beat eggs, sugar, and salt together till whites and yolks are thoroughly blended. Heat milk, and when almost boiling pour it gradually into egg mixture, stirring. Flavour to taste (vanilla, finely grated orange or lemon rind, soluble coffee). Pour into a 2½ pint oven-proof dish and stand this in a shallow tin with hot water coming half-way up sides of dish. Cook for about 1½ hours at Gas Mark ½, 250°F. The custard's ready when it's set and a knife blade slid into it midway between centre and side comes out clean. Remove baking dish from pan of water, and leave custard to cool.

One-stage Ice Creams

Peggy's Ice Cream

> 2 eggs
> 1 small can evaporated milk
> 3 tbsp. caster sugar
> vanilla essence

Separate egg yolks and whites. Whisk the whites in a bowl. Beat contents of a small size can of evaporated milk – if it has been boiled and chilled beforehand (see p. 44) so much the better. Then whisk into the milk the sugar, egg yolks, and two or three drops of vanilla essence. Fold in beaten egg whites. Pour into freezing tray with fridge set at its coldest and leave till set; when it's ready to eat serve with one of the sauces at the end of this chapter.

Vanilla Ice Cream

> 2 cups whipping cream
> ½ cup sifted icing sugar
> ½ tsp. vanilla essence
> 1 egg white

Whip cream and add vanilla and sugar. Beat egg white and when stiff fold into cream. Pour into freezing tray in refrigerator and freeze till set.

Fruit Ice

> 2 *cups thick fruit purée*
> ½ *cup sifted icing sugar*
> 1 *cup whipping cream or ½ cup chilled evaporated milk*

Whip cream or evaporated milk till stiff. Add sugar to the purée, then fold this into the cream. Pour into freezing tray, and leave till set.

Note: The purée can be canned, or make your own using fresh fruit or drained canned fruit. (About 1 lb. fruit stewed and sieved yields ½ pint purée). You can use apricots, blackcurrants, bananas, apples, strawberries, raspberries etc.

Chocolate Mousse

This isn't cheap, but it's dead simple and *fabulous*! Break 8 oz. sweetened chocolate into pieces, put them in a bowl, and stand that in a pan of boiling water. When melted, blend in ½ pint whipped double (or whipping) cream. Place in small dishes and chill in fridge.

Do It Yourself Yoghurt

Sweet and fruity yoghurt makes super desserts for children, who mostly love it. Buying one pot per person is pricy, though, so what about buying a yoghurt-maker? You can buy yoghurt-makers that do the job splendidly. *Or* make it one of these two ways, one using a wide mouthed thermos flask, the other not. You need a little bought yoghurt to start with, but thereafter your own home-made can act as 'starter'.

Yoghurt Version 1

> 1 *pint milk*
> 1 *tbsp. best plain yoghurt (the Bulgarian kind is excellent if you can get it)*
> 1 *tbsp. Casilan (a milk protein powder sold by good chemists)*

Just bring the milk to slightly below boiling point, then leave to cool to blood heat. Mix the yoghurt with the Casilan, stir this into the milk and pour into a thermos, prewarmed by pouring in hot water. Leave overnight, and by the morning – it's yoghurt! If it *should* come out rather runny, it's still working, so just whip it up and put it back again for a couple of hours. Once you've made your own yoghurt, of course, you can whip different fruit purées into it, flavouring it with coffee essence or drinking chocolate powder. Or serve it with sugar and chopped mixed nuts, or with a blob of honey.

(*Note:* If you can't get Casilan, use 2 tbsps. of yoghurt instead of one.)

Yoghurt Version 2

> 1 *pint milk*
> 1 *tbsp. yoghurt*

Bring 1 pint milk to almost boiling, then allow it to cool to blood heat. Test with a thermometer or by dipping in your finger. If you can hardly feel the heat, it's about right. Stir in 1 tbsp. of yoghurt then put the mixture in front of hottest heater or open fire you have – or right up against a radiator. In a few hours, from 3–6 depending on temperature of heater or radiator, the result is yoghurt.

Whichever way you make your yoghurt, you can use it for the recipes on pps. 137, 138, 160, 168, 169.

Devon Apples

> 1 *lb. sharp cooking apples*
> *little water*
> ½ *pint cider*
> *sugar to taste*
> *lemon rings to garnish*

Chop apples without peeling and simmer in only a little water till tender, then liquidise or rub through sieve. Add the purée to the cider. Taste, and stir in required sugar while apple mixture is warm enough to dissolve it. Serve really cold. Garnish with lemon rings.

Apple Almond Pudding

> 5 *oz. butter or margarine*
> 12 *level tbsp. caster sugar*
> ¾ *cup ground almonds*
> 1 *large egg*
> 1½ *lb. cooking apples, peeled, cored and shredded*
> 6 *level tbsp. demerara sugar*
> 1 *rounded cup breadcrumbs*
> 2 *tbsp. chopped blanched almonds*

Cream 4 oz. of the butter or margarine with the caster sugar. Beat in the ground almonds and egg till light and fluffy. Melt remaining fat in a shallow oven dish. Add and mix in the apples, brown sugar and breadcrumbs. Press evenly into the dish, and cover with almond mixture. Sprinkle with chopped almonds. Cook for 6 hours (Gas Mark ¼, 200°F.) in the centre of the oven. Serve cold, decorated with whipped cream.

Baked Apples

> 6 *large cooking apples*
> 6 *tsp. sugar*
> 2 *oz. butter*
> 6 *tsp. golden syrup*
> *a few sultanas and raisins (optional)*

Wash, dry and core apples. Lightly score round centre of apple using small knife, so skin doesn't split during cooking. Place apples in heatproof dish or tin, and fill each centre hole with 1 tsp. sugar, 1 tsp. syrup and a knob of butter (plus dried fruit, if using it). Put about ⅛ inch cold water at the bottom of baking dish. Bake halfway down oven (Gas Mark 4, 350°F.) for 30–40 minutes or till apples are soft when tested with skewer. Lift onto heated dish. Remove top half of skin if liked. Pour syrupy liquid from baking tin over apples. Serve with cream.

Apple Rice Pudding

Put a layer of creamy rice pudding (leftover home-made or canned) at the bottom of a buttered dish. Cover this with apple purée. Add another layer of rice pudding. Heat in a moderate oven (Gas Mark 4, 350°F.) for about 25 minutes.

Minted Orange and Grapefruit

  3 *grapefruit*
  2 *medium oranges*
  2 *rounded tsp. chopped mint*
  few small sprigs of mint

Cut each grapefruit in half horizontally, and remove fruit from each half by cutting around fruit segments with a sharp pointed knife. Place fruit in basin, reserve grapefruit shells. Remove pith from fruit with scissors. Peel oranges, separate segments, remove outer pith and peel and place segments in basin with grapefruit. Add chopped mint and mix well. Leave in a cool place for at least 1 hour, so that flavours blend. Just before serving, pile fruit into grapefruit shells, and decorate each with a small sprig of mint.

Desert Dessert

  10 *seedless tangerines*
  1 *cup chopped dates*
  ½ *cup chopped walnuts*
  ½ *cup lemon juice*
  6 *tbsp. vanilla sugar*
  powdered cinnamon

Peel and divide tangerines into segments. Put in a bowl with everything except cinnamon. Chill. Sprinkle with cinnamon just before serving.

Note: Vanilla sugar is caster sugar that's had a vanilla pod stored in it. If you have none, use ordinary caster sugar and a drop or two of vanilla essence.

Frosty Fruit Cups

You can make any mixture of diced fresh or canned fruits seem special if you do this. Just beat up the white of a large egg on a plate. Dip the rims of dessert glasses first in this, quickly, then in sifted icing sugar. Put glasses in refrigerator for the 'frost' to freeze. Have the diced fruit also chilling in refrigerator. When the time comes, spoon fruit into crispy edged glasses.

N.B. If there's any egg white and sugar left, and you've some white grapes, treat these the same way as the glass rims and refrigerate. Pop a grape or two on each fruit cup.

Grape Cream

> 4 *cups seedless white grapes*
> 1 *cup yoghurt*
> ½ *cup soft brown sugar*

Mix everything. Refrigerate for two hours or more, and serve in sundae glasses. Serve with shortbread biscuits or squares of Butter Pudding (see p. 131).

Chocolate Pear Delight

> 1 *large* (1 *lb.* 1 *oz.*) *can pear halves*
> 2 *rounded tbsp. drinking chocolate*
> 10 *tbsp. golden syrup*
> *milk*
> 1 *packet chocolate-flavour dessert whirl*

Drain pears, then slice them and divide the pieces between 6 small glasses. Place drinking chocolate in a small saucepan and add 5 tbsp. golden syrup, and stir over a moderate heat until sauce boils. Simmer for 4 to 6 minutes stirring occasionally, until sauce is thick

and dark. Leave to cool. Place remaining syrup in a measuring jug
Make up to ½ pint with milk. Pour into a basin, add contents of
packet of dessert whirl and whisk until light and creamy. Leave to
thicken slightly, spoon over pears in goblets. Top each goblet with
chocolate sauce. Serve immediately.

Stewed Fruit with Munchy Macaroons

The stewed fruit can be any sort – hot or cold. As for the chewy
texture macaroons to serve with them – make them this way:

>4 *cups quick cooking oatmeal*
>2 *cups brown sugar*
>1 *cup salad oil*
>2 *beaten eggs*
>1 *tsp. salt*
>1 *tsp. almond essence*

The night before, mix together oatmeal, brown sugar and salad oil.
Next morning, mix in beaten eggs, salt, almond essence. Drop
from a teaspoon onto a greased baking sheet, and bake at Gas
Mark 3, 325°F., for 15 minutes. Remove promptly when done.

Blackcurrant Cap Pudding

>15 *oz. can blackcurrant pie filling*
>6 *oz. luxury margarine*
>12 *tbsp. caster sugar*
>3 *large eggs*
>6 *heaped tbsp. S.R. flour*
>1 *tsp. baking powder*

Well grease a 2 pint pudding basin. Place 2 tbsp. of pie filling in
bottom of basin. Put all other ingredients into a mixing bowl, and
beat with a wooden spoon for 2–3 minutes or until mixture is very
smooth (even quicker with electric mixer). Spread mixture on top
of pie filling. Cover tightly with greased foil. Put in steamer, or
stand in a large saucepan, half filled with boiling water, with a

tight fitting lid. Steam or simmer for about 1¾ hours. Heat up remaining pie filling and serve as a sauce with pudding. (Other pie fillings can be used the same way.)

Steamed Sponge Pudding basic (for 6)

USING BAKE MIX

8 heaped tbsp. of the mix
1 egg
and fold in 8 rounded tbsp. S.R. flour
1–2 tbsp. warm water or milk

STARTING FROM SCRATCH

4 oz. margarine
8 level tbsp. caster sugar
2 eggs
2 cups S.R. flour
1–2 tbsp. warm water or milk

USING BAKE MIX

Put mix into basin. Beat in egg and warm water or milk, then fold in flour.

FROM SCRATCH

Cream margarine and sugar. Beat in the beaten eggs and warm water or milk. Fold in the flour.

Then, grease a 2 pint basin, prepare a piece of double greaseproof paper to cover it, and grease the centre of the paper where it touches the pudding. Put the sponge mixture into the greased basin. Cover with prepared paper, and tie firmly with string. Steam gently for 2–2½ hours. Turn onto a heated plate, and serve immediately, with custard.

For Jam Cap Pudding – same but put 2 tbsp. jam at the bottom.

For Syrup Pudding – put 2 tbsp. golden syrup at the bottom.

For Spotted Dick – add 2 oz. currants, having washed and dried fruit.

For Pineapple Pudding, blend in 2 tbsp. finely chopped pineapple.

For Chocolate Sponge, use 1 oz. flour less; add 1 oz. cocoa.

For Ginger Sponge – add 2 level tsp. ground ginger.

Sweet Spud Dumplings

Follow recipe for potato dumplings (p. 185) but add sugar to taste (about 2 level tbsp.). Serve with hot jam, honey or syrup. If you like cook the dumplings in milk, not water, then flavour the milk with jam, honey or syrup to make the sauce.

Crumble Puddings

Whenever you don't know what else to give them, there's always good old crumble. You can use your Pastry Mix on p. 39 to make a crumble topping, or use the Keeping Crumble (p. 42). Use it, thinly or thickly sprinkled according to taste, to top stewed fruits, or canned pie fillings. Cook $\frac{1}{2}$–$\frac{3}{4}$ of an hour near the top of a fairly hot oven (Gas Mark 6, 400°F.).

CHAPTER SIX

Picnics and Parties

PICNICS

Al Fresco Omelettes

Yes – omelettes are grand on a picnic! Make them in the usual way with a filling of cheese, bacon and onion, mushroom and tomato, or whatever you fancy. Potato omelettes seasoned with salt, pepper, and a dash of sweet paprika are good, too. Pack each omelette individually in foil. Or put the omelette between slices of thickly buttered rye or French bread.

Sandwiches

Sandwiches, always a standby, can be made the night before to save a rush the following day. Well wrapped in foil and stored in refrigerator or cold larder, they'll keep moist and fresh for up to 12 hours.

Just for a change, make picnic sandwiches with a variety of breads – malt bread, fruit bread, granary bread etc. Secret of interesting sandwiches is to introduce plenty of new flavours. Try chopped celery, cream cheese and peanut butter; meat and Marmite, or meat and dripping; chocolate spread and banana; chopped walnut and banana; hard-boiled egg with mayonnaise and curry powder.

Terrine

A terrine makes great picnic fare, if you take along a crusty French loaf, butter and pickled cucumbers, gherkins, or pickled onions.

This recipe couldn't be easier – specially if you ask the butcher to mince the meats for you.

1 lb. fatty pork
1 lb. lean veal (or pork)
½ lb. pig's liver   } minced
3 oz. streaky bacon
small clove garlic, crushed
small onion chopped
beaten egg
salt and pepper

Set oven at Gas Mark 3, 325°F. Turn mixture into terrine or greased loaf tin. Stand tin in roasting pan half full of water and cover the terrine with foil. Cook about 1¼ hours, or till the sides have shrunk slightly and the top feels firm. If you want the terrine really firm, put a weight on top to press it while it's cooling.

Lamb Loaf

1 shoulder lamb
1 clove garlic
½ pint dry white wine
2 tsp. dried thyme (or sprig of fresh)
½ tsp. dried rosemary (or fresh)
½ tsp. dried basil
1 tsp. salt
1 small bay leaf

Trim surplus fat off lamb. Put the sliced, peeled garlic at the bottom of a casserole, and place the shoulder of lamb on it. Put in everything else and cook slowly (Gas Mark 4, 350°F.) till the bone can easily be removed from the meat. Allow about 45 minutes per lb., and a minimum 2 hours if lamb weighs less than 3 lb.

Place boned meat in dish just large enough to take it. Put plate and weight on top and leave in cold place to cool as rapidly as possible. Remove weight, cover with foil, and store in refrigerator. To serve, turn out of dish and slice thinly. Use liquid for soup or stock.

Brown Bread Salad called 'panzanella' by the Italians

This salad travels well in a tightly lidded plastic container. Keep it in the refrigerator till the last moment.

> 6 *slices day-old brown bread, cut roughly in cubes*
> *enough stock or water (cold) to cover*
> 1 *clove crushed garlic (optional but it makes it twice as good)*
> *sprinkling of fresh or dried basil*
> 1 *medium onion, finely chopped*
> 3 *tomatoes (chopped and skinned)*
> 1 *tbsp. chopped parsley*
> *black pepper, salt*
> 2–3 *tbsp. olive or other oil*
> 1 *tbsp. vinegar*
> *a few capers and/or chopped gherkins*

Pour water or stock over the bread, and leave till the bread's all mushy. Meanwhile, mix in a bowl the onion, garlic, herbs, tomatoes, vinegar and oil. Squeeze out the bread to remove excess moisture, then mix it in well with all other ingredients. When completely blended, put in refrigerator.

Take it on your picnic to eat with cold meats, canned tuna or salmon. If you like, mix the fish with the rest of the salad.

Savoury Tomato Squares

> 2 *cups S.R. flour*
> 1 *rounded tsp. salt*
> 2 *oz. margarine*
> 1 *level tsp. mixed dried herbs*
> 1 *standard egg*
> 5 *tbsp. milk*
> 6 *firm tomatoes*
> 12 *level tbsp. Cheddar cheese*

Prepare a hot oven (Gas Mark 7, 425°F.). Grease a small baking sheet or a 10 inch × 6 inch shallow tin. Place flour and salt in a bowl.

Add margarine cut into small pieces, and rub in with the fingertips until mixture resembles fine breadcrumbs. Stir in mixed herbs. Beat egg and add to mixture with 5 tbsp. of milk, mixing with a fork to a soft dough. Turn out onto a floured board and knead lightly. Press dough evenly into tin, and mark into 12 squares. Place tomatoes in a bowl and cover with boiling water. Leave for 1 minute, drain, peel, then cut in halves. Place 1 tomato half, cut side downwards, in centre of each square. Grate cheese and sprinkle a thick layer over tomatoes. Bake just above centre of oven for 20–25 minutes until risen and golden brown. Leave to cool in tin for a few minutes, then cut into squares. Transport it to your picnic in the tin.

Cheese and Sultana Flan

> *make Cheese Pastry to line a* 10 *inch flan case* (see p. 39)
> 16 *tbsp. strong Cheddar cheese*
> 4 *tbsp. sultanas*
> 1 *level tbsp. flour*
> 1 *cup and* 2 *tbsp. of milk*
> 3 *eggs*
> *salt and pepper*

Roll out cheese pastry and use it to line 10 inch flan tin. Coarsely grate cheese into case. Sprinkle with sultanas. Place flour in bowl. Beat milk and eggs together then gradually beat into flour till all ingredients are well blended. Season to taste. Pour mixture over the cheese. Cook flan on centre shelf of heated oven for 45 minutes or till filling is set and golden. Serve cold with a tub of coleslaw.

PARTIES

Party Dips

Sweet and Savoury Dips are fun at a party. Serve crisps, Ritz crackers and melba toast to dip into the savoury ones, semi-sweet biscuits – round and finger shapes – to dip into the sweet.

Cream Cheese Dips

A good supply of cream cheese is the starting point for all kinds of dips. To a basic Dip Mix of 8 oz. cream cheese, and 2–3 tbsp. milk, add any of the following:

> *plenty of chopped cucumber and 8 tsp. Catalina dressing*
> *2 oz. chopped ham and 1 dstsp. chopped onion*
> *4 oz. drained shrimps and ½ tsp. chopped parsley*
> *1 tbsp. Thousand Island Dressing and a clove of crushed garlic*
> *1 tsp. curry powder and 4 oz. chopped shrimps*
> *1 tbsp. coconut*
> *1 tbsp. thin honey and 3 oz. finely chopped nuts*
> *2 oz. canned chopped pineapple*
> *1 tbsp. raspberry jam*

Yoghurt Dips

Sardine and Yoghurt Dip

> *1 carton yoghurt*
> *2 cans sardines (skinless and boneless for preference)*

Put the sardines, drained of oil, into a mixing bowl, add the yoghurt and mix to a smooth cream. Intriguing flavour – and the sharpness of the yoghurt cuts the oiliness of the sardines. You can add lemon juice if you like.

Nice with fingers of toasted brown bread.

Spring Dip

Mix 2 cartons of natural yoghurt with ½ packet Spring Vegetable Soup. Leave the dip at least 2 hours. Serve with young carrots, cut in quarters.

Curry Dip

Grate half an onion and one unpeeled dessert apple into a cartonful of natural yoghurt. Flavour with a level tsp. of curry powder, half a level tsp. of turmeric, 2 level tbsp. chopped piccalilli and one tbsp. of thick cream. Serve sliced red and green apples with the dip.

Cool Cucumber Dip

Grate half a cucumber, sprinkle it with salt, and leave it for half an hour to extract some of the moisture. Dry it, and add it to a carton of natural yoghurt, along with 1 level tbsp. chopped mint. Season with salt and freshly ground black pepper. Serve the dip with cucumber slices.

Pickle Dip

Stir 2 tbsp. of sweet pickle and 1 tbsp. raisins into a carton of natural yoghurt.

Other Dips

Cheese Dip

Using a packet of cheese sauce, make it up with half the usual amount of milk. Add chopped hard-boiled egg, pinch cayenne pepper, and 2 tsp. Worcester sauce.

Cranberry Dip for sausages at party

1 *level tbsp. cornflour*
1 *tbsp. white vinegar*
2 *rounded tbsp. cranberry relish*

Blend cornflour with vinegar in small saucepan, stir in the cranberry relish, bring it to the boil stirring continuously, then cook for one more minute. Serve hot or cold.

Sardine Spread

½ *tsp. anchovy paste*
4 *sardines skinned and crushed*
¼ *cup finely chopped onion*
2 *chopped hard-boiled eggs*
¼ *cup (2 oz.) creamed butter*
grated rind 1 lemon
lemon juice to taste
2 *dstsp. minced chives*

Blend everything together. Use to top biscuits or toast fingers, or as sandwich filling.

Creamy Almond Roll

6 *oz. cream cheese*
1½ *oz. Kraft Danish Blue Cheese*
2 *oz. ham (chopped)*
8–10 *stuffed olives or 4 pickled onions (chopped)*
1 *cup chopped almonds*

Beat cream cheese until smooth. Add the Danish Blue Cheese and mix thoroughly. Then stir the chopped ham and chopped olives or pickled onions into the cheese mixture. Place almonds under grill or in a hot oven until pale brown. Shape the cream cheese mixture into a roll, then coat it in the toasted nuts. Roll up in kitchen foil or greaseproof paper and chill thoroughly in a refrigerator, or leave overnight in a cool place. Next day cut in slices ⅛ inch thick, and serve on rounds of brown and white bread, or on water biscuits.

Cheese Snaps

½ *cup flour*
2 *oz. butter*
4 *oz. flavoured processed cheese spread (i.e. bacon or cheese and onion spread)*

Mix all together. Shape into neat roll, wrap in waxed paper, and put in refrigerator. When firm, slice as for biscuits, place on an ungreased baking tray, and bake at Gas Mark 6, 400°F. for 10–15 minutes.

Savoury Pinwheels

For 20–24 pinwheels.

> 4 oz. streaky bacon
> 1 medium sized onion
> 2 cups Scone Mix (p. 42)
> salt and pepper
> 5 tbsp. milk
> 2–3 oz. Cheddar cheese
> little fat for cooking

Prepare a moderate oven (Gas Mark 5, 375°F.). Grease 2 baking sheets. Remove rind from bacon, and chop coarsely. Peel onion and chop. Place bacon and onion in small pan with fat and cook slowly, till the onion softens and is golden. Turn onto a plate and leave to cool. Add some salt and pepper to scone mix, and make into a dough with the milk. Turn onto a floured board, and knead lightly. Roll out scone dough, and trim to a rectangle about 14 inch by 12 inch. Spread bacon and onion mixture over the dough, taking it right out to the edges. Cover this with grated cheese, and sprinkle with salt and pepper (use a little cayenne if your family like stronger flavouring).

Starting from a short side, roll up dough, Swiss roll fashion; with a sharp knife, cut into ½ inch slices. Place slices on baking sheets, cut side downwards, and a little apart, to allow room for spreading. Bake in centre of oven for about 20 minutes. Serve warm or cold.

Sue's Huckle Buckle

> ½ lb. butter
> 2 tbsp. golden syrup
> ½ a large can condensed milk

10 *level tbsp. brown sugar*
2 *tsp. powdered ginger*
a handful of sultanas
vanilla essence
chopped walnuts
2 *packets plain sweet biscuits*

Put first 5 ingredients in a saucepan and boil for 10 minutes stirring all the time. Add sultanas, vanilla essence, and a few chopped walnuts. Crush the biscuits, not too fine. Stir them into the 'fudge' mixture, then press into an oblong tin to a depth of about ¾ inch. Cut into small squares or fingers when set (small, because this is *very* rich).

Holiday Apricot Cookies

They look pretty and taste good. For 25–30 cookies.

1 *can* (15½ *oz.*) *apricot halves*
4½ *cups desiccated coconut*
1 *small can condensed milk*
¾ *cup almond nibs or chopped blanched almonds*

Drain juice from apricots, then place fruit on soft kitchen paper to remove excess moisture. Chop apricots into small pieces. Mix with coconut and condensed milk. Roll into small balls and toss in prepared nuts. Put balls on a baking tray and leave to set. Place each ball in a small paper sweet case and spear with a cocktail stick, then pierce the sticks into a couple of oranges.

Crisp Marshmallow Squares

For approx. 20 small squares.

2 *oz. butter*
½ *lb. marshmallows*
4 *cups Rice Krispies*

Put Rice Krispies in a greased bowl. Melt butter and marsh-mallows in a bowl in a saucepan of hot water. Remove from the heat, stir till smooth and creamy, then pour it over the Rice Krispies. Stir well. Press the mixture in a greased 7¼ inch square shallow tin. Allow to set, then cut into neat squares.

Chocolate Orange Fudge

¼ lb. chocolate, cut into pieces
2 oz. butter
4 tbsp. tinned evaporated milk
grated rind 1 orange
1 lb. sifted icing sugar

Melt chocolate and butter together. When melted, blend in evaporated milk. Flavour with orange rind and stir well. Then blend in icing sugar. Work mixture till stiff but smooth. Press into a lightly greased tray, and leave to set.

Party Squares

Really rich for big occasions, when time is at a premium. Line a rather shallow, 7¼ inch square baking tin with non-stick paper, leaving flaps to overlap the sides for easy lifting.

4 oz. plain biscuits (Marie, Rich Tea, etc.)
2 oz. digestive biscuits
6 tbsp. chopped walnuts
4 tbsp. seedless raisins
3½ oz. butter
2 level tbsp. caster sugar
3 tbsp. golden syrup
6 tbsp. cocoa, sifted

Roughly crush all biscuits. Coarsely chop shelled walnuts and seedless raisins, and mix with the biscuits. Cream together the butter, caster sugar and golden syrup. Beat in cocoa, and work in the biscuits, walnuts and raisins. When the ingredients are well mixed, press evenly into the tin and leave overnight in a cold place. Frost the next day with the chocolate fudge icing, on p. 237.

Nut Fudge

> 3 oz. packet cream cheese
> 2 cups icing sugar
> ½ tsp. vanilla
> ½ cup chopped nuts
> pinch salt
> 2 squares semi-sweet chocolate

Blend together everything except chocolate, then melt chocolate in a bowl placed in a pan of hot water over gentle heat, and stir into the cream cheese mixture. Press into a buttered tin, mark in squares, and chill till firm.

Coffee Kisses

> 2 cups Suet Mix, p. 40 (or 3 heaped tbsp. suet, and 6 heaped tbsp. S.R. flour)
> 6 tbsp. caster sugar
> 1 tbsp. instant coffee powder, dissolved in 1 tbsp. water
> 1 large egg, beaten

Mix together suet mix (or suet and flour) and sugar. Stir in egg and coffee liquid, mix well, and knead mixture lightly. Roll into small balls, and place on greased baking trays, leaving a space between each one. Bake for 10–15 minutes, Gas Mark 5, 375°F. When cold, sandwich together in pairs with coffee butter icing (see p. 239).

CHAPTER SEVEN

Any Time Snacks

COLD SNACKS

Quick Gazpacho

Satisfying summer snack, served with crispy fresh bread.

> $\frac{1}{4}$ *cucumber*
> I *green pepper*
> I *small onion*
> I *small clove garlic, crushed (optional)*
> I *can (10$\frac{1}{2}$ oz.) condensed tomato soup*
> I$\frac{1}{2}$ *soup cans water*
> 3 *tbsp. salad oil*
> 2 *tbsp. wine vinegar*
> $\frac{1}{4}$ *tsp. Marmite*
> *little salt and pepper*
> *sliced lemon*

Thinly slice cucumber, finely chop green pepper and onion, crush garlic. Mix all ingredients together except sliced lemon. Cover. Place in refrigerator 4 hours or overnight. Stir gently. Serve in chilled bowls, and garnish with sliced lemon.

Pilchard and Potato Salad
(in proportions to suit yourself)

Pilchards, cold boiled potatoes, a minced onion or shallot, oil and vinegar, salt and pepper, a few capers or other pickles, mayonnaise, sliced hard-boiled eggs, lettuce.

Separate the fish into flakes. Mix it in a large salad bowl with all
the ingredients except the eggs and lettuce, tasting as you go and
using about twice the amount of potatoes as fish. Blend and stir
well, using as much oil and vinegar as you wish, and then just a
little mayonnaise to make it creamy. Let it stand for two or three
hours so that flavours blend, and then arrange lettuce leaves around
the side and decorate with the eggs and anything else you like to use.
Slices of beetroot and cooked peas may be added, and it is a wonderfully elastic dish to make for a large gathering.

Mayonnaise Snacks

Using your store cupboard mayonnaise (see p. 47) or a good,
bottled variety, you can turn all sorts of things into tasty snacks.

For Egg Mayonnaise

Hard boil the eggs, and when cool, shell, halve them, and cover
with mayonnaise. Garnish with something bright, so that it looks
as good as it tastes.

Fish Pyramids

Use cooked cod or any white fish of similar texture. Flake it into tiny
pieces with your fingers. Mix it with mayonnaise, capers, and a
small can drained shrimps. Shape into little pyramids and serve as
cold as possible with salad and crisps.

Nut and Raisin Slaw

> 1 *firm-hearted white cabbage* (*medium size*)
> $\frac{1}{2}$ *cup mixed peanuts and raisins*
> 1 *dessert apple*
> 1 *cup salad cream mixed with* $\frac{1}{2}$ *cup milk* (*or to suit taste*)
> *salt and pepper*

Shred the cabbage very finely. Mix in the nuts and raisins. Core
the apple, but do not peel it. Chop it roughly, add it to the slaw

with the salad cream, and salt and pepper to season. Serve with cold meats.

STOVE TOP AND GRILL SNACKS

Tyrolean Cheese Soup

> 4 cups grated cheese (best if you include some Parmesan or Gruyère)
> 8 tbsp. chopped spring onions or chives
> ½ lb. margarine
> 1 cup flour
> 2 pints hot water (or half milk and half water)
> salt and black pepper

Melt margarine, take saucepan off heat, and blend in flour and seasoning. Very gradually add hot water mixing with wooden spoon till very smooth. Keep stirring till the mixture is back to bubbling. Then put on a close fitting lid, and cook on lowest possible heat (preferably on an asbestos mat) for 20 minutes. Give occasional stir with wooden spoon. Just before serving, add the grated cheese and stir till melted. Check seasoning and when it's just right pour the soup into bowls and garnish each portion with chopped spring onions or chives. Serve with chunks of brown bread.

Jiffy Soup

> 2 onions
> 4 sticks celery
> 2 oz. margarine
> 4 tomatoes
> 8 oz. any leftover cooked meat (ham, chicken, beef)
> 2 cloves garlic, crushed
> good pinch mixed herbs
> seasonings to taste
> 1 pint water

1 *pint milk*
16 *oz. can butter beans (optional, but adds extra bulk)*
2 *heaped tbsp. plain flour*

Prepare and chop all vegetables. Fry the onions and celery gently, till they're tender but not brown. Add tomatoes and meat, diced, along with all seasonings, milk, and all but ½ cup water. Bring to the boil and simmer a few minutes. Add butter beans, then blend flour with remaining water and add to soup. Bring to boil, stirring, then lower heat and simmer 5 minutes before serving.

Quick Corn Soup

1 *can creamed sweet corn*
1 *cup milk*
1 *heaped tbsp. flour*
1 *pint water*
1 *onion*
salt and black pepper

Peel and chop onion and put it, and the corn, in a pan with the water. Simmer till onion is tender, then blend in flour with a little of the cold milk and add to soup, together with rest of milk. Bring to boil. Simmer 4 minutes. Season with salt and black pepper, and garnish with paprika and chopped parsley.

Corn on the Cob

When it's in season and not too expensive, sweet corn on the cob makes a splendid snack – either with loads of butter, pepper and salt, or with this *plus* ham, bacon, or sausages. And here's the way to cook the corn cobs, if you're not sure that everyone will be sitting down at the same time.

Put the cobs in a large saucepan of cold water. Don't add salt, but for 6 ears of corn put in 3 tbsp. vinegar and 3 tbsp. white sugar. Cook ordinarily, bringing to the boil and letting it bubble for 6 or 7 minutes. From then on, just keep the water hot, and don't remove corn till it's wanted for eating. It will stay at just-right eating point for ages. And, if necessary and providing the corn hasn't been removed, the water can get cold and be hotted up again, without ill effects.

Corn Stirabout

> 1 *medium onion, chopped*
> 1 *rasher bacon per person*
> 1 *can whole kernel sweetcorn*
> *grated cheese*

Fry onion. Fry bacon and chop. Warm corn and stir together, with everything else. Sprinkle over with grated cheese and pop under grill to brown.

Irish Tiddy

A snack that makes a tasty breakfast dish, too.

> 6 *large ripe tomatoes*
> 4 *eggs, beaten*
> *hot buttered toast*
> 2 *oz. butter*
> ¼ *tsp. fresh basil leaves (optional)*
> *salt and black pepper*

Slice tomatoes and fry in the butter for 3 minutes. Add sweet basil, if you like it, then add the beaten eggs. Turn heat to very low, stir mixture well with wooden spoon, and leave to cook a further 2 minutes. Season with salt and black pepper. Don't overcook or it will spoil. Take pan off heat while the eggs are still slightly runny. The heat in pan will finish cooking it. Stir, then pile on hot buttered toast.

Spanish Eggs

> 1 *large can baked beans*
> 6 *eggs*

3 *tomatoes, finely chopped*
3 *tbsp. grated cheese*

Heat beans thoroughly and turn into an oven dish that's able to fit under the grill. Crack in the eggs, season, sprinkle with chopped tomato and grated cheese. Grill till egg whites are set. To make the snack more substantial, add bacon or sausages.

Brown Eggs

6 *large eggs*
3 *tbsp. soy sauce*
2 *oz. butter*
cold water as required

Boil eggs for five minutes, leave them in cold water till cool enough to handle, then shell. Melt butter in small pan, add soy sauce, and then the whole eggs. Cook for 6–7 minutes basting the eggs all the time till they're evenly browned. Allow to cool, then serve cut in slices on bed of fried savoury rice.

Cheese and Liver Scramble

6 *oz. margarine or butter*
12 *oz. calf's or lamb's liver (cut into small pieces)*
6 *large slices white bread (crusts removed)*
8 *eggs*
4 *tbsp. milk*
salt and pepper
8 *oz. grated Cheddar cheese*

Melt half butter in frying pan and gently fry liver pieces, turning, for 8–10 minutes until cooked. Remove to a plate and keep warm. Fry bread in same pan, adding more margarine or butter as necessary. Beat together eggs, milk and seasonings. Melt remaining butter in saucepan, add egg mixture and cook gently, stirring, until just creamy. Add liver, remove from heat and stir in cheese. Serve on the fried bread.

Cottage Rarebit

> 6 *slices toast*
> 6 *hard-boiled eggs*
> 12 *oz. cottage cheese*
> 6 *oz. mushrooms fried in butter or margarine*
> *salt and black pepper*

Mash eggs thoroughly, add to the cottage cheese, and season. Add mushrooms and pile mixture on toast. Put into a very hot oven (Gas Mark 8, 475°F.) for a few minutes, till slightly browned.

Cheese Fingers

Cut any firm cheese into finger shapes. Sprinkle with cayenne pepper (unless your kids can't stand anything 'hot'). Wrap a thin rasher of bacon round each finger, and skewer with a wooden tooth-pick – or skewer several 'fingers' together onto a metal meat skewer. Grill till the bacon is crisp, and serve straight away, either with grilled tomatoes or salad, or on fingers of toast.

Cheese Puff

> 12 *tbsp. grated cheese*
> 1 *cup soft breadcrumbs*
> 2 *eggs*
> 1 *oz. soft butter*
> *salt and pepper*

Put cheese, breadcrumbs and butter in frying pan and stir together as they all heat through. When almost melted, add well-beaten seasoned eggs. Carry on stirring till the mixture can be pushed into a very soft, puffy shape. Spoon a portion onto each plate, and serve with salad.

Ham and Apple Grill

> 6 *small apples*
> 3 *oz. butter*
> 6 *slices cooked ham, about ¼ inch thick*
> 6 *slices cheese*

Remove rack from grill pan and prepare a moderate grill. Peel apples, cut each apple in half and scoop out core. Melt butter in grill pan. Add apple halves and turn in melted butter, grill them, cut sides uppermost, for 5 minutes. Then remove apples from pan, put in ham slices and place 2 apple halves on each slice of ham, cut sides downwards. Grill for a further 5 minutes. Place cheese slices on top of apple halves and grill until golden brown and bubbling. Serve immediately with chipped potatoes or crisps.

Macaroni Balls

Make up the macaroni mixture beforehand, then the snack's easy to prepare when you want it.

> 2 *oz. macaroni*
> 1 *oz. butter*
> 1 *heaped tbsp. flour*
> 12 *tbsp. grated cheese*
> ¼ *pint hot milk*
> 1 *egg, separated*
> *a little made mustard*
> *pepper and salt, dried breadcrumbs*

Wash macaroni in cold water and boil till tender. Drain and chop finely. Put butter into a saucepan, add the flour and cook till it bubbles, then withdraw from the heat and beat in milk till smooth. Gently boil, stirring, until thick. Add seasoning, cheese, macaroni and yolk of egg. Leave to get cold, then flour your hands and on a floured board make up the macaroni mixture into balls or rolls. Brush over with white of egg, lightly beaten, coat with breadcrumbs, and fry in boiling fat.

Bread and Cheese Omelette

> 1½ *cups milk*
> 1½ *cups soft breadcrumbs*
> 12 *tbsp. grated cheese*
> 9 *eggs, well beaten*
> *salt and pepper*
> 2 *oz. butter*

Warm milk, and soak breadcrumbs in it until they've absorbed all the liquid. Add well beaten eggs and seasoning to taste. Melt butter in frying pan, and when it's smoking hot pour in egg mixture. Stir well for a second ot two.

Then wait a few moments till surface begins to set. Sprinkle on the grated cheese, and when this starts softening, cut into portions. (It's best to cook this mixture, which serves 6, in halves.)

Spicy Sardine Slices

> 2 *cans sardines*
> *pinch cayenne pepper*
> *squeeze of lemon juice*
> 6 *slices bread*
> *butter*
> 4 *tsp. brown sugar*
> 2 *tsp. dry mustard*
> *vinegar*

Cut crusts off bread, and fry in melted butter, turning over when one side is crisp, but keeping the pan covered the rest of the time. Mash the sardines with some of their own oil, cayenne, and a squeeze of lemon juice. Spread fried bread with a mixture of sugar and mustard bound into a 'paste' with the vinegar. Pile the sardine purée on this, then put under grill for a few moments.

Kipper Rolls

Cut fingers of bread and butter, and lay strips of kipper fillets on each one. Roll them, keep in place with a wooden toothpick or cocktail stick. Dip quickly in and out of a mixture of beaten egg and milk. Deep fry. Super with any salad – try chopped celery and apple, with a French dressing.

Stick Snacks

Spike a selection of whatever's available on skewers (steel knitting needles work a treat, too, if they're *real* steel!).

For instance, skewer pieces of lamb, kidney, liver or fish, along with bits of onion, tiny whole tomatoes, green pepper, celery. Cubes of salami or luncheon meat are good, too, and so's bacon and sausage. Exotic combinations are pineapple and ham, or whole cooked prunes or slices of banana wrapped in bacon. Whatever you choose, load each skewer with enough to satisfy appetites, brush with oil or melted fat, season, and put under a preheated hot grill, turning occasionally till everything is cooked. Eat with bread and butter, or scoop each skewer full onto a bed of rice or mashed, buttery potato. Remember, if one thing takes longer than the others to cook, it should either be par-cooked beforehand or put on the skewers earlier.

Fried Rice

> *2 oz. margarine*
> *4 rounded tbsp. chopped spring onion or chopped onion*
> *2 rashers bacon, rind removed and chopped*
> *4 oz. prawns, shrimps or tuna*
> *1 lb. long grain rice, cooked and cooled*
> *1 small (4 oz.) packet frozen peas, cooked*
> *2 eggs, standard, made into omelettes and cut into strips*
> *seasoning*

Melt margarine in large frying pan and gently sizzle prepared onion and bacon for 10 minutes. Add all remaining ingredients and seasoning. Heat through completely and serve hot.

Savoury Drop Scones

Follow the recipe for Drop Scones (see p. 200) but substitute salt and pepper, to taste, for the sugar, and add 1 rounded dstsp. grated Parmesan. The egg and milk mixture can be spiked with a dash of tomato sauce and of Worcester sauce (slightly reducing milk to allow for this extra liquid).

Cook in exactly the same way as the sweet drop scones.

Savoury Fritters

Follow recipe on p. 145 or 146 for Sweet Fritters, using stock, tomato or vegetable juice as liquid, rather than milk or water. Use the batter to coat onion rings, sausages, fish fillets, savoury sandwiches, parboiled vegetables.

Speedy Rarebit

Take out your Cheese Mix (p. 45) from the refrigerator. Toast bread normally on one side, and very lightly on the other. Spread the lightly-done side with butter, and top each slice with 3 tbsp. of the Mix, spreading to cover the edges so that they won't burn. Grill till bubbling.

Variation is to spread a pulp of canned tomatoes, or slices of fresh tomato, under the cheese topping.

Cup Rarebit

Grate and thinly flake a strong cheese into a breakfast cup till 3 parts full. Pour on boiling water. Leave to stand for 10 minutes while you make a salad or get out the cutlery. Then pour off the water and the cheese will be like thick cream at the bottom. Serve on hot toast, adding salt and pepper to taste.

Potato Dumplings

Use your prepared potato dumpling mix, or follow recipe on p. 45 halving ingredients. Form into 'torpedo' shapes, slide gently into a large pan of briskly boiling water. Cook about 4 at a time *only*, because they swell (if you want to cook more simultaneously, use two pans). The dumplings sink to the bottom at first, but then come up and float. They cook in 10–12 minutes. Test by removing one, and cutting through the centre, and if done it will be light and springy. When ready, drain, cut into slices and serve with stews, casseroles, minced beef etc. Leftover cooked dumplings make a good supper dish (see next recipe).

Supper Quickie

Cut leftover potato dumpling (or ordinary dumplings) into pieces. Fry them with chopped bacon and onion. When cooked, stir in one beaten egg per person. When the eggs are cooked, the snack's ready to serve.

OVEN-COOKED SNACKS

Oven-bake Sandwiches

> ¼ *lb. strong flavour cheese, diced*
> ¼ *lb. melted butter*
> 1 *cup milk, warm*
> 1 *large egg yolk*
> 4 *tbsp. flour*
> *bread as required* (*stale is fine*)
> *salt and black pepper*

Blend together flour, melted butter and salt and pepper, and very gradually add warm milk, stirring. Cook over gentle heat, stirring with wooden spoon till very thick. Take pan off heat, blend in diced cheese and egg yolk, and mix well. Cut thick slices of bread and spread them with cheese mixture. Grease baking sheet and place slices on it. Bake in a hot oven (Gas Mark 7, 450°F.) for about 10 minutes. (For adults, try dipping bread slices in white wine before spreading with the topping.)

Baked Potatoes

Scrub potatoes, prick, wrap in aluminium foil, and bake in a pre-heated fairly hot oven (Gas Mark 6, 400°F.) till cooked.

Large potatoes take about 1½ hours, medium potatoes about ¼ less. When cooked, fold back foil showing top potato surface. Make diagonal cuts in potato top, and slosh on butter and chopped chives or cream cheese.

Egg and Green Bean Bake

> 1 *large can whole green beans* (*or equivalent in fresh cooked beans*)
> 6 *eggs*
> 6 *tbsp. single cream*
> *salt and freshly ground black pepper*

Spread the beans over the base of an ovenproof dish and sprinkle them with salt. Break the eggs onto the beans and run a tbsp. of single cream over the yolk of each egg. Sprinkle with salt and pepper. Bake the eggs in a fairly hot oven (Gas Mark 6, 400°F.) for 12 to 15 minutes. The whites should be just set and the yolks still soft.

Independent Bacon and Egg

Independent, because the bacon and egg look after themselves in the oven. A good idea for breakfasts, too.

Grease fireproof dish or tin. Take rinds off bacon and place rashers in bottom of dish. Crack eggs into a saucer, and slide into dish on top of bacon. Chipolata sausages and halved tomatoes can also be added. If mushrooms are wanted, put a knob of butter in the cup of each one. Bake at Gas Mark 5, 375°F. for about 30 minutes or till eggs are set.

Frank Beans

A dish that doesn't pretend to be anything grand.

> 12 *frankfurters* (*the small size*)
> 1 *lb. baked beans*

1 tbsp. flour
1 tsp. mustard
¼ cup water
¼ cup tomato ketchup
2 tbsp. vinegar
2 tsp. sugar

Cut frankfurters in half lengthwise and put in shallow baking dish, or deep frying pan. Add beans to them. In a small pan, blend flour and mustard to smooth paste with water. Add other ingredients, then heat and stir till it thickens. Pour it over the sausages and beans and cook gently for 30 minutes either on top of, or in, the oven (Gas Mark 6, 400°F.). Serve with a green salad.

Hazelnut Bake

4 oz. mashed potato
4 oz. ground hazelnuts
1 cup grated cheese
½ lb. fried tomatoes
1 small onion, grated
chopped parsley
salt and black pepper

Mix together all the ingredients, except the cheese, and season. Put into a greased baking tin, sprinkle with cheese and bake for 25 minutes in a fairly hot oven (Gas Mark 6, 400°F.).

Savoury Fillings for Pastry Cases

Using a 10 inch ready baked pastry case, any of the following fillings can give you speedy hot or cold tarts:

Fish filling – 2 cans of tuna (or prawns, or shrimps) blended with Cheese Sauce (see p. 46).

Kids' curry filling – using recipe on p. 66.

Savoury ham filling – as much ham (or bacon) as you like mixed into the White Sauce (p. 49), seasoned well with salt, pepper, a little dry mustard.

Bacon and corn filling – canned, cream style sweetcorn blended with pieces of lightly fried bacon.

Bread Pizza

> 6 *slices bread,* $\frac{1}{2}$ *inch thick*
> 1$\frac{1}{2}$ *oz. butter, melted*
> 1 *medium* (15 *oz.*) *can tomatoes, well drained*
> *salt and pepper*
> *pinch mixed herbs*
> 4 *oz. can anchovy fillets, drained*
> 16 *tbsp. cheese, grated*
> *stuffed olives*

Remove crusts from bread, brush with melted butter and place on greased baking sheet, or sheets. Divide tomatoes between bread slices, and sprinkle with salt, pepper and mixed herbs. Arrange anchovy fillets on top and cover with grated cheese. Garnish with olives. Bake near the top of a fairly hot oven (Gas Mark 6, 400°F.) for 15 minutes. Serve hot with green salad.

Quick Pizzas

> 1 *small onion*
> 2 *rashers streaky bacon*
> 1 *dstsp. cooking oil*
> 1 *medium* (15 *oz.*) *can peeled tomatoes*
> 2 *level tbsp. cornflour*
> $\frac{1}{2}$ *level tsp. mixed dried herbs*
> *salt and pepper*
> 2 *cups Scone Mix*
> 12 *tbsp. Cheddar cheese, grated*
> 2 *stuffed olives*

Grease 2 baking sheets. Peel and finely chop onion. Remove rind and bone from bacon, cut into small pieces. Place oil in a small saucepan, add onion and bacon and cook gently for 5 minutes without browning onion. Add contents of can of tomatoes. Blend cornflour with a little water and add to saucepan with the dried herbs. Bring to boil, stirring, and cook gently for 10 minutes stirring occasionally. Taste and season well with salt and pepper. Allow to cool. Make up Scone Mix as on p. 202, using salt and pepper instead of sugar, and leave in a cool place for 5 minutes. Turn out on to a floured board and divide mixture into 6. Shape each piece into a round and roll out thinly to a circle. Place circles on baking sheets. Spoon the sauce over the circles to within $\frac{1}{4}$ inch of edges. Sprinkle with grated cheese, place a piece of sliced olive in the centre of each round. Bake just above centre of a moderately hot oven (Gas Mark 4, 350°F.) for 10 minutes. Serve hot.

Note: to speed things up even more, roll out scone dough to an oblong, spread topping over surface, and cut into squares when it's cooked.

CHAPTER EIGHT

Cakes and Bakes

EAT NOW

Best Brownies

Moist, 'more-ish' chocolate squares – cut them small, because they're rich.

  4 oz. unsweetened chocolate
  ⅔ cup cooking oil
  4 eggs
  2 cups sugar
  2 tsp. vanilla essence
  1½ cups sifted plain flour
  1 tsp. baking powder
  1 tsp. salt
  1 cup chopped nuts
  icing sugar

Heat oven to Gas Mark 4, 350°F. Grease an oblong pan. Combine chocolate and oil in small saucepan. Heat over low heat until chocolate is melted. Remove from heat and cool. Beat eggs thoroughly. Beat in sugar and vanilla. Add chocolate mixture and blend well. Sift flour, baking powder and salt together into mixture, and blend well. Stir in nuts. Spoon into prepared pan and bake for about 30 minutes or until sides are firmish but centre is still a little soft. Cool in pan. Sift icing sugar over top, before cutting into squares.

Hokey Kokey Biscuits

Recipe given to me by an Australian mum. She says that even someone what *can't* cook can manage these. And she's right!

> ½ *lb. butter or margarine*
> 1½ *cups brown sugar*
> 2 *heaped cups white S.R. flour*
> 2 *dstsp. milk*
> 2 *dstsp. golden syrup*
> 2 *tsp. bicarbonate of soda*

Melt syrup and milk together. When melted and cooled down add bicarbonate of soda. Beat till frothy. Cream butter and sugar, then add to it first the frothy mixture and then the flour. Roll into balls, press with a fork onto a well greased baking sheet leaving plenty of room for the biscuits to spread. Cook in a slow oven (Gas Mark 2, 300°F.) for about ½ hour.

Oatmeal Crunch Biscuits

> 8 *oz. margarine*
> 16 *tbsp. soft brown sugar*
> 2 *cups quick porridge oats*
> 2 *cups coconut*
> 2 *cups flour*

Put oats, coconut and flour into a bowl. Melt together margarine and brown sugar, and pour this over the oats mixture. Blend well, tip into a greased tin and bake for 25 minutes in a moderate oven (Gas Mark 5, 375°F.).

Dutch Shortcake

> 6 *oz. butter*
> 6 *heaped tbsp. demerara sugar*
> 2 *eggs, separated*
> 6 *heaped tbsp. S.R. flour*

1½ oz. *glacé cherries, chopped*
1½ oz. *walnuts, chopped*
½ oz. *candied peel, chopped*

Cream butter and sugar until light, beat in egg yolks then stir in flour. Press evenly into a greased, shallow oblong tin. Blend egg whites with fork until slightly frothy, add nuts and fruit. Spread over mixture in tin. Bake at Gas Mark 3, 325°F. for about 55 minutes. Cut into fingers or squares whilst still warm. After cooling for 10 minutes, remove from tin.

Australian Crisp

1½ *cups crushed cornflakes*
1½ *cups flour*
1½ *cups coconut*
6 oz. *margarine*
rind and juice of one lemon
icing sugar

Soften margarine. Beat all ingredients into warm margarine. Bake in flat tin for 20 minutes in a moderate oven (Gas Mark 4, 350°F.). Blend lemon juice and rind with icing sugar and quickly smooth this over cake surface while still warm.

Pineapple Slices

1 lb. *drained, crushed pineapple*
2 *cups porridge oats*
8 *heaped tbsp. S.R. flour*
8 oz. *margarine*
1½ *cups soft brown sugar*

Mix oats with flour, rub in margarine with fingertips. Stir in sugar. Press half mixture into an oblong, shallow tin. Spread pineapple over this, cover with remaining mixture. Press down well. Bake on centre shelf of fairly hot oven (Gas Mark 6, 380°F.) for 25-30 minutes. Mark into slices. Leave to cool.

Peanut Squares

So easy, the kids can make them.

> 8 *tbsp. clear honey*
> 8 *rounded tbsp. peanut butter* (*crunchy*)
> 6 *oz. broken biscuits, crushed*
> 2–3 *oz. seedless raisins*

Place honey and peanut butter in saucepan. Stir over gentle heat for 8 minutes till well blended together. Remove from heat, stir in the raisins and lightly crushed biscuits. Press mixture into oblong, shallow tin. Leave in cool place till set. Cut into squares.

Sultana Munchies

> 1 *cup plain flour*
> 1 *level tsp. baking powder*
> 1½ *level tsp. powdered cinnamon*
> ¼ *level tsp. salt*
> 1 *packed cup sultanas*
> ¾ *cup shelled walnuts, chopped*
> 2 *large eggs*
> 14 *level tbsp. caster sugar*
> 1 *oz. butter, melted*
> *icing sugar*

Lightly grease and line an oblong shallow baking tin. Sift together the flour, baking powder, cinnamon and salt. Blend in the sultanas and nuts. Whisk together the eggs and sugar until pale and fluffy, stir in the melted butter. Stir in the dry ingredients. Turn into prepared tin. Bake in a moderate oven (Gas Mark 4, 350°F.) for about 50 minutes. Cut into squares while still warm. Serve dusted with icing sugar. Makes about 24.

Favourite Krispies

> 8 *cups Rice Krispies*
> 6 *level tbsp. golden syrup*

2 *level tbsp. sugar*
2 *level tbsp. margarine*
few drops almond or vanilla essence

Put syrup, sugar and margarine into pan, and bring to boil, stirring all the time. Boil for 1 minute then stir in essence to taste. Put the Rice Krispies into a bowl, and pour the hot mixture over them. Mix well with a wooden spoon, and turn into greased tin. Press down well. Allow to stand in a cool place for ½ hour, or till cold. Cut into 18 squares.

Savoury Nut Biscuits

Something different for the tea-table.

1 *cup chopped nuts (salted or unsalted)*
2 *cups flour*
a pinch salt (if nuts are unsalted)
1 *tbsp. butter, finely shredded*
1 *tsp. baking powder*
milk for mixing

Blend nuts, flour, salt and finely shredded butter. Add baking powder and mix thoroughly. Use enough milk to make a firm paste, and knead on floured board for a few moments. Roll thinly, cut into shapes, and place on well buttered baking sheet. Cook in a slow oven (Gas Mark 2, 300°F.) till golden.

No-Bother Buttercake

The day you discover the kids have rampaged through the biscuit tin is *always* the day the shops are closed and you're rushed off your feet. However hectic things are, though, you can find time to knock up a batch of these delicious crunchy biscuits (come to that, press-gang a child to do it for you).

6 *heaped tbsp. granulated sugar*
½ *lb. butter (or margarine, but it's less good)*
2 *cups plain flour*

Melt butter over gentle heat, and when liquid and just bubbling, remove from heat, toss in other ingredients, and mix together. Within moments, it will come away from the edge of the pan in a soft moist ball. Pick this up, plop it into a lightly greased 7 inch square tin. Cook for 20 minutes at top of moderate oven (Gas Mark 5, 375°F.). By then it should be goldy brown – but it will still look bubbly and a bit un-set. Ignore this. Go ahead and take it out of the oven. Leave it to cool in tin, and mark into squares or fingers before it's quite cold. If you're lucky enough to have any left over, store them in an airtight tin.

One-stage Fruit and Nut Cake

Quick to 'knock up' when you're pushed for time – and nicest when eaten really fresh.

> 6 *oz. luxury margarine*
> 12 *level tbsp. caster sugar*
> 3 *eggs*
> 5 *tbsp. milk*
> *pinch salt*
> 3 *cups S.R. flour*
> 1 *level tsp. mixed spice*
> 10 *tbsp. mixed dried fruit and nuts (put them about half and half or according to taste)*

Grease and line an 8 inch round cake tin with greased greaseproof paper. Put all ingredients into a bowl, and beat well with a wooden spoon or in a mixer till well mixed and light. Turn into prepared tin. Bake on centre shelf of moderate oven (Gas Mark 4, 350°F.) for 1½–1¾ hours or till well risen and golden brown. When cooked, a skewer inserted into centre comes out clean.

Rough Robin Cake

A cut-and-come-again cake.

> 8 *heaped tbsp. ground rice*
> 3 *cups flour*

4 oz. soft lard
6 level tbsp. granulated sugar
⅔ cup currants
⅔ cup raisins (stoned and chopped)
1 tbsp. chopped candied peel
½ tsp. caraway seeds
pinch salt
½ pint milk
1½ tsp. baking powder

Mix flour, ground rice and salt. Rub in lard. Stir in sugar, caraway seeds, fruit, and peel and (last of all) baking powder. Mix to a fairly stiff dough with milk. Bake in moderate oven (Gas Mark 5, 375°F.) in a greased baking tin for 20–25 minutes. When cooked, cut in pieces, sprinkle with caster sugar and serve hot (though it's O.K. cold, too). If you do not like caraway seeds, these can be left out.

Family Bun Ring

3 cups S.R. flour
4 level tbsp. golden syrup
4 level tbsp. black treacle
4 level tbsp. thick-cut orange marmalade
12 tbsp. sultanas
½ pint milk; oil or melted fat

Brush an 8½ inch ring tin with oil or melted fat. Place flour in a bowl, and make a well in the centre. Measure syrup and treacle carefully, levelling off spoon with the back of a knife, and making sure there is none on underside of spoon. Add to flour, with marmalade and sultanas. Mix in about half the milk and beat until smooth. Blend in remaining milk. Pour into tin. Bake in a low oven (Gas Mark 3, 325°F.), just below centre of oven for 1¼–1½ hours when the ring should have stopped bubbling. Test by pressing with your fingers – if cooked, the ring should spring back. Leave to cool in tin for 30 minutes. Run a knife around between loaf and tin to loosen edges, then turn out and leave the bun ring to cool on a wire rack. Serve sliced and buttered.

Fast Fruit Cake

So called because it's quick to mix, though the actual cooking time's lengthy.

> 1½ *cups plain flour*
> 1 *tsp. baking powder*
> ½ *tsp. salt*
> 1 *tsp. mixed spice*
> ¾ *cup fine dark brown sugar*
> ¾ *cup ground almonds*
> 3 *eggs*
> 5 *oz. softened butter*
> 2 *tbsp. milk*
> 4 *cups mixed dried fruit*
> *whole or sliced almonds* (*optional*)

Sift flour, baking powder, salt and mixed spice into bowl. Add sugar, ground almonds, and mix. Make a well in centre and put in eggs, butter and milk. Mix till smooth. Stir in dried fruit. Put into 8 inch cake tin lined with greased greaseproof paper and smooth top flat. If liked, cover top with almonds. Bake in a fairly cool oven (Gas Mark 1, 275°F.) for about 3 hours.

Date and Nut Bread

> 1 *lb. chopped dates*
> 1½ *cups boiling water*
> 4 *cups plain flour*
> 1½ *tsp. bicarbonate of soda*
> 1 *heaped cup granulated sugar*
> 2 *eggs*
> 2 *oz. butter*
> 1 *cup chopped nuts*

Put chopped dates in basin. Add bicarbonate of soda and boiling water. Allow to cool. Rub fat into flour. Add sugar and nuts. Beat eggs and add to flour mixture with dates and water. Put into a greased 2 lb. loaf tin, and cook 1½–2 hours (the first half-hour at Gas Mark 4, 350°F., then lowered to Gas Mark 3, 325°F.)

Quick Banana Bread

1½ *cups plain flour*
2½ *tsp. baking powder*
½ *tsp. salt*
½ *cup chopped nuts*
⅓ *cup shortening*
⅔ *cup sugar*
2 *slightly beaten eggs*
1 *cup mashed banana*
1 *cup mixed candied peel and fruit*
¼ *cup raisins*

Sift flour, baking powder and salt. Add nuts. Blend. Beat shortening till creamy; slowly add sugar, beating till fluffy. Add eggs, and beat till thick. Add flour mixture and bananas alternately, blending after each addition. Fold in fruit. Grease a 2 lb. loaf tin and bake in a moderate oven (Gas Mark 4, 350°F.) for 60–70 minutes. (Cover top of loaf with foil once it's the right golden-brown shade.) Serve fresh, sliced and buttered.

Two-way Sponge

With this mixture, you can make a Swiss roll *and* a single layer sponge to top with fruit and cream. Or it will make two sponge layers to sandwich together.

3 *eggs*
7 *tbsp. caster sugar*
2 *heaped and* 1 *level tbsp. plain flour*
pinch baking powder, sifted with flour

Whisk eggs and sugar together in a warm bowl till thick and frothy. Fold in flour and baking powder. Put half the mixture into a greased, floured 7½ inch diameter sponge tin, and spread the other half over an oblong tin lined with greased greaseproof. Cook in a very hot oven (Gas Mark 8, 475°F.) allowing 7 minutes for the Swiss roll and 10 minutes for the round sponge. When the Swiss roll sponge is still warm, spread on the jam and roll the sponge carefully.

Simple Sponge using Bake Mix

> 5 *heaped tbsp. Bake Mix (p. 41)*
> 5 *rounded tbsp. S.R. flour*
> *just enough liquid (water, milk, fruit juice or undiluted fruit squash) to make a batter that drops from the spoon*

Grease and flour 2 7½-inch sandwich tins. Set oven at Gas Mark 5, 375°F. Blend all ingredients together and turn into prepared tins. Bake about 20 minutes in preheated oven.

Drop Scones

> ¾ *cup Bulk Batter Mix (p. 43)*
> 1 *dstsp. caster sugar*
> 1 *small egg beaten into sufficient milk to make total egg and milk ¼ pint (or just over half a cup)*

Gradually add sugar to the dry mix, then beat in the beaten egg and milk. Grease a heavy bottomed frying pan or griddle pan and get it good and hot (if you haven't made drop scones before, you'll soon find out just the right heat). Cook for about 2 minutes on the first side, or till golden brown, then turn and cook the second side same way. The batter in the middle should then be set. Wrap in a folded tea towel till ready to eat – remembering that they're nicest warm.

Tea Time Scones starting from scratch

> 2 *cups S.R. flour*
> *pinch salt*

3 oz. margarine
4 tbsp. granulated or caster sugar
milk to mix

Mix flour and salt, rub in margarine. Add sugar, stir in milk to make a soft dough. Turn onto a floured board, roll out to an inch thick. Cut into rounds, place on greased baking tray. Brush with milk. Bake at Gas Mark 7, 425°F. for 10–15 minutes. Serve warm, split and buttered. (If liked, add 4–6 tbsp. dried fruit to the above mixture.)

(For scones using basic mixes see following recipes.)

Scones 1 using Multi-Purpose Mix

1¾ cups Multi-Purpose Mix as on p. 42
good pinch salt
4 tbsp. sugar
milk

Blend dry ingredients, and bind with milk to soft but not sticky consistency. Roll out to ½ inch thick, cut into rounds or triangles, and bake on trays towards the top of a hot oven (Gas Mark 7, 425°F.) for about 10–15 minutes. (For variations see p. 202.)

Scones 2 using Bake Mix

A non-traditional but very good scone can be made using your Bake Mix (p. 41). To each heaped tbsp. of Bake Mix, allow 5 rounded tbsp. S.R. flour. Work the flour into mix with a fork. Then blend in just enough milk to make a moist but pliable dough. Turn onto a well floured baking sheet, pat with hands to ¾ inch thickness and cut out scone rounds on the baking sheet, or pat into a ring and cut into triangular slices. Bake at Gas Mark 7, 425°F. for 10–15 minutes. Eat hot, or re-heat by putting into loosely wrapped foil and heating in a very hot oven 10 minutes.

CAKES AND BAKES

Scones 3 using Scone Mix

Using 2 cups Basic Scone Mix (p. 42), blend 1 tbsp. caster sugar, 1 beaten egg, and enough milk to combine with eggs to give ¼ pint liquid. Mix to a soft but not sticky dough, adding whatever liquid is needed (use remainder to brush over the scone tops). Turn onto a floured board, and knead lightly for a smooth dough. Cut into rounds, or press down into one large round, brush with milk, and place on a greased baking sheet. Bake near the top of a hot oven Gas Mark 7, 425°F. for 10–15 minutes till well risen, cooked through and golden brown.

Scone Variations

Whichever way you make your scones, there are plenty of changes you can ring. As follows:

Fruit scones – add dried fruit to taste.

Cheese scones – leave out sugar, but add 2 oz. cheese, grated (*not* suitable for Bake Mix Scone recipe).

Wholemeal scones – use half white and half wholemeal flour when making up mix or when making scones from scratch (as on p. 200).

Griddle scones – same recipe, but lightly grease a griddle or thick frying pan on low-medium setting. When heated, cook scones on it till brown underneath (5–7 minutes). Repeat on second side.

Crunchy Topped Squares

Children love the colourful 'gooey' topping.

TOPPING

    2 *tbsp. glacé cherries*
    3 *oz. margarine*
    1 *rounded tbsp. golden syrup*
    ¾ *cup porridge oats*

12 *tbsp. desiccated coconut*
4 *level tbsp. demerara sugar*

CAKE

4 *oz. butter or margarine*
8 *tbsp. caster sugar*
2 *standard eggs*
4 *heaped tbsp. S.R. flour*

Thoroughly grease a shallow oblong tin and line the bottom with greased greaseproof paper. To make topping: Coarsely chop cherries. Place margarine and golden syrup in a saucepan and melt over a low heat. Remove from heat and stir in oats, coconut, demerara sugar and glacé cherries.

To make cake: Cream butter and sugar together until light and fluffy. Beat eggs together and add gradually to the butter and sugar, beating after each addition. (Or make the base using Bake Mix, following Sponge recipe on p. 200.) Sift flour, and fold into creamed mixture, till well blended to a soft, dropping consistency. Level mixture over the tin and spread with the topping. Place in centre of moderate oven (Gas Mark 4, 350°F.) and bake for 50 minutes until it's golden and the bubbling has stopped. Cool. Cut into 15 squares.

Cocoa Cake

5 *heaped tbsp. Bake Mix (p. 41)*
5 *rounded tbsp. S.R. flour*
2 *level tbsp. cocoa*
2 *level tbsp. golden syrup*
2 *tbsp. milk*
1 *level tbsp. granulated sugar*

Prepare a moderately cool oven (Gas Mark 3, 325°F.). Brush a round 8 inch cake tin with oil or melted fat, and line with double thickness of greased greaseproof paper. Fold flour into Bake Mix. Place cocoa in small saucepan. Measure syrup carefully, levelling

off with spoon. Add to cocoa with milk. Stir over low heat til
mixture thickens and boils. Stir till cool. Fold cocoa mixture into
cake mixture. Spoon into tin and level top. Sprinkle with granulated
sugar. Bake in centre of oven for about 1½ hours. Test by pressing
with fingers. If cooked, cake should spring back, have stopped
bubbling and begun to shrink from sides of tin. Turn out, remove
paper, and cool on wire rack.

Mincemeat Topper

Drained canned fruit mixed with brown sugar can be spread at the
bottom of the tin in place of mincemeat, or use your favourite jam.
Serve with canned cream or custard.

> *make up a sponge mixture, following one of the recipes*
> *on pp.* 199 *or* 200
> 8 *oz. mincemeat*
> *grated rind of* ½ *lemon* (*optional*)

Grease an oblong baking tin. Spread the mincemeat on the bottom
of the tin. Sprinkle with lemon rind, if used. Make up the sponge,
as per recipe. Spread carefully over the mincemeat to cover. Bake in
a Gas Mark 5, 375°F., oven for 15–20 minutes until the sponge is
just firm to the touch and drawing away from the sides of the tin.
Turn out carefully onto a heated plate so that the mincemeat is
at the top.

Note: Put apple slices over the mincemeat too, if you like.

Crisped Coffee Cake

> 1 *tbsp. butter*
> ½ *cup crushed cornflakes*
> ¼ *cup brown sugar*
> 1 *level tsp. cinnamon*
> 1 *or* 2 *tsp. chopped walnuts*
> ½ *tsp. vanilla essence*

5 heaped tbsp. Bake Mix (p. 41)
5 rounded tbsp. S.R. flour
2 tsp. powdered coffee
plus a little water or milk to make the batter 'dropping'
consistency

Put 1 tbsp. butter into an 8 inch round cake tin and put into oven to melt fat. Mix crushed cornflakes, brown sugar, cinnamon, chopped walnuts. When fat melts, pour this into mixture and stir well, adding vanilla essence. (Use melted fat remains in tin to brush it round and grease it.) Prepare a sponge, folding flour into the Bake Mix, and adding liquid (as on p. 200). Then add powdered coffee. Pour half this sponge batter into the greased tin. Sprinkle with half the cornflake mixture. Cover with the rest of batter, then sprinkle on remaining crunch mixture. Bake in moderate oven (Gas Mark 5, 375°F.) for 55–60 minutes.

Caraway Crunchies

Using one or other of your short pastry mixes (see pp. 39, 230), blend in some caraway seeds. Roll out, cut into rounds, and bake on a greased sheet in a very hot oven (Gas Mark 8, 475°F.) for a few minutes, till crisp. When cold, sandwich rounds together with cream cheese flavoured with a dash of paprika, garlic or chopped chives – even all three together.

(This is a good way, too, of using up leftover short pastry.)

Date Loaf

3 cups Basic Scone Mix (p. 42)
8 oz. stoned dates
4 tbsp. orange squash
milk
2 level tbsp. granulated sugar

Prepare moderately hot oven (Gas Mark 6, 400°F.). Brush a 2 lb. loaf tin with oil or melted fat. Cut up dates. Place orange squash in a measuring jug and make up to ¼ pint with milk (don't worry if it seems a little curdled – it's O.K.). Add dates and milk to scone mix: stir with fork till just mixed. Sprinkle with sugar. Bake in centre of oven for 1–1¼ hours till golden brown and cooked through. Remove from oven, turn onto wire rack, and leave to cool. Serve sliced and buttered, when very fresh.

Banana Honey Buns

1 *tbsp. honey*
2 *large bananas*
2 *cups Basic Scone Mix (p. 42)*
milk (or beaten egg) and demerara sugar to glaze

Warm the honey, mash bananas, and mix together. Add to scone mix with a little milk to form a soft but not sticky dough. Roll out ½ inch thick on lightly floured board, and cut in triangles. Place on greased baking sheets. Brush tops with beaten egg, or milk, and sprinkle with demerara sugar. Bake towards top of very hot oven (Gas Mark 8, 475°F.) for 7–10 minutes. Makes about 16 buns.

Apple and Almond Fingers

2¼ *cups of Multi-Purpose Mix, p. 42 (or 2 oz. margarine and*
    7 heaped tbsp. S.R. flour rubbed together)
2 *grated or finely chopped raw apples*
4 *heaped tbsp. demerara sugar*
2 *eggs, beaten*
¾ *cup blanched almonds*

To the Mix (or margarine and flour mixture) add the grated apple, sugar and beaten eggs. Put into an oblong tin, lined with greased greaseproof paper. Top with blanched almonds. Bake for about 25–30 minutes in the centre of a moderate oven (Gas Mark 5, 375°F.) till firm, but still slightly springy when pressed. Cuts into about 12 fingers. Eat while fresh.

Toddy Cake

I make this in a deep baking tin, and it's just the thing for cold days when the kids bring in ravening appetites and a friend apiece. It's cheap, too, and mixes up so easily that there's no need to get out the electric mixer even if you *have* one.

> 2 *packed cups of cooked, mashed potato (if you haven't any leftovers, the instant kind made like the packet says, is fine)*
> 3½ *cups raisins, sultanas, or currants (or a mixture of all or some of them)*
> 2 *scant cups shredded suet*
> 1 *cup sugar*
> *pinch nutmeg*
> 2 *eggs*
> 4 *cups S.R. flour*

Mix the mashed potato, dried fruit, suet, sugar and nutmeg all together. Then work in the eggs, lightly beaten. Gradually blend in the flour to make a light, spongy dough, press in a greased baking tin to about 2 inch thick, and bake at the centre of a moderately hot oven (Gas Mark 6–7, 400–425°F.) for 45–55 minutes, or till golden brown on top, firm but slightly springy. Serve deliciously, indigestibly, hot. Some like it spread with butter, or drizzled over with hot syrup, pudding-fashion. It won't be quite so good the next day, eaten cold. But if you quickly damp the outside with cold water, and heat it fast for 5 minutes at the top of a very hot oven, that will freshen it almost like new.

Assorted Jiffy Buns

Even the best-organised Busy Mums tend suddenly to run out of every cake and biscuit in the house. To fill the tea-time gap, these Jiffy Buns can be made speedily using your Bake Mix (see p. 41). They're nicest eaten fresh, so make just what you think will be wanted *now*.

1½ *cups S.R. flour*
1 *cup Bake Mix*

Just fold the flour into the Mix, and work into a light dough. Pull pieces off and roll with your hands into small balls (the above amount makes about 10 buns). As you roll them, place on a wooden board. Now add variety. You can make a small finger-hole at the top of each bun, and fill it with jam. Others can have holes filled with chocolate chips, and be sealed by moulding the dough back over the hole again. A portion of the dough can be worked in with ground ginger, cinnamon or mixed spice. Another can have crushed cornflakes kneaded in, and be rolled in extra cornflakes. This only takes minutes to do. Then place the buns on a well-greased and floured baking tray, as far apart as possible, because they spread a little. Bake for 12–15 minutes in a preheated oven (Gas Mark 6, 400°F.). If you make them slightly smaller to give more buns, they take a little less time.

Note : Keep your eye on them – once done, they'll burn quickly if neglected.

BAKE NOW – EAT LATER

Apple Loaf

This is a splendid keeper – in fact, is best left for 2 or 3 days before eating, and can keep in an airtight container for up to 6 or 7 weeks. So it's perhaps worth making two or three while you're about it.

3 *oz. soft margarine*
⅔ *cup S.R. flour*
¼ *tsp. bicarbonate of soda*
¼ *tsp. baking powder*
½ *tsp. each cinnamon and ground ginger*
3 *level tbsp. sugar*
1 *cup mixed dried fruit*
1 *rounded cup apple purée*

Cream margarine. Mix in flour, bicarbonate of soda, baking powder and spices with a fork. When smooth, stir in sugar and dried fruit. Then add apple purée, till the mixture is blended and 'sludgy'. Tip it into a greased, 1 lb. loaf tin. Bake just above the centre of a hot oven (Gas Mark 7, 425°F.) for ½ hour. Then reduce heat to warm (Gas Mark 3, 325°F.) and cook 1 hour more. Don't turn out of tin for 30 minutes.

Note : This cake virtually doesn't rise at all, so don't expect it to. It comes up a fraction, but as it cools, reduces to its previous level. It is wonderfully moist, and if you eat it the first day (which you shouldn't) you'll find it hard to cut anything but thick, uneconomical slices!

Mincemeat Quickie

A 'tray-bake' that can't really go wrong, unless you put in salt instead of sugar, or something of the sort.

> 6 *oz. margarine*
> 4 *tbsp. brown sugar*
> 2 *tbsp. white sugar*
> 2 *good cups porridge oats*
> 4 *level tbsp. flour*
> 2 *eggs*
> mincemeat to taste (*about* 1 *lb. or more if you like it* really thick)

Blend the oats and flour. Melt together the margarine, brown sugar and white sugar. Remove from heat and pour into this the oats and flour. Add the eggs, well beaten. The mixture should be a little stiff, but you can add a tablespoon or so of milk if it seems to need it. Spread two-thirds of the mixture in a greased 10 inch × 6 inch baking tray, cover with the mincemeat, and then spread on another, sparser, layer of the mixture. Bake about 20 minutes fairly near the top of a moderately hot oven (Gas Mark 6–7, 400–425°F.). When cool cut into squares.

Batch Biscuits

There's no doubt that home-made biscuits come a whole lot cheaper than the packet kind. And while you're having a biscuit-making session, it pays to make several traysful and flavours from one basic mixture.

FOR THE BISCUITS
  4⅔ *cups plain flour*
  1¼ *lb. luxury margarine*
  3⅓ *cups caster sugar*
  4 *egg yolks*
  4 *dstsp. cold water*

FOR FLAVOURINGS
  4 *level tsp. instant coffee*
  6 *tbsp. currants*
  4 *rounded tbsp. desiccated coconut*
  4 *oz. finely chopped walnuts*

Rub margarine into flour, then stir in sugar. Beat egg yolks and water lightly together, and mix with dry ingredients to a smooth, firm dough. Shape into a long roll on a floured board. Divide this roll into 4 equal portions. Into each of the four portions work a different flavouring. Then roll each portion out thinly on a lightly floured surface and cut into 2½ inch rounds. Place these, slightly apart, on greased floured baking sheets, brush over with milk and sprinkle with caster sugar. Bake for 15–20 minutes in a preheated, very moderate oven (Gas Mark 3, 325°F.) about a third of the way up the oven. When removed, cool on wire tray before putting into airtight tins.

Yorkshire Parkin

A deliciously moist, substantial cake. In some parts of the North it's traditional fare at Bonfire Night parties.

  16 *tbsp. medium oatmeal*

3 *heaped tbsp. flour*
5 *heaped tbsp. soft brown sugar*
2 *tsp. ground ginger*
½ *tsp. bicarbonate soda*
pinch salt
10 *level tbsp. treacle*
¼ *lb. butter or margarine*

Mix dry ingredients together. Put treacle and butter (or margarine) in a pan, and heat until just melted. Stir into dry ingredients and mix well. If necessary, add a little milk to make a soft dropping consistency. Spoon into a well-greased 2 lb. loaf tin and bake at Gas Mark 3, 325°F. for ¾–1 hour. Keep for 2–3 days in a tin before eating.

Gingerbread

Super moist gingerbread that keeps some time in an airtight tin (or eat it hot with custard, as a pudding). Cook 45 minutes at Gas Mark 4, 350°F.

1½ *cups plain white flour (or half white and half wholemeal)*
1 *tsp. mixed spice*
pinch salt
1 *tbsp. ground ginger*
4 *tbsp. sultanas*
2 *tbsp. chopped peel*
3 *tbsp. brown sugar*
1 *egg*
1 *tsp. bicarbonate of soda*
½ *cup milk*
4 *oz. butter or margarine*
8 *tbsp. golden syrup or honey*

Sift flour, mixed spice, salt and ginger into mixing bowl and blend. Add sultanas, peel, brown sugar. Melt fat and syrup but don't allow to become hot. Mix soda and milk till soda dissolves. Add, with egg, to dry ingredients, and mix till well blended. Pour into a very well-greased ring tin and bake about 40 minutes in a moderate oven (Gas Mark 4, 350°F.) till cooked through but still springy in centre. Cool for 10–15 minutes, still in tin, before turning onto rack. When cold store in airtight box. (This gingerbread takes to deep freezing, too.)

Overnight Cake

    1 *cup All Bran breakfast cereal*
    1 *cup brown sugar*
    1 *cup mixed dried fruit*
    1 *cup milk*
    1 *cup S.R. flour*

Put the All Bran, sugar and mixed fruits into a bowl. Pour on the milk and leave overnight (or at least a couple of hours). Next day thoroughly blend in the flour, put in well greased 2 lb. loaf tin, and bake at the centre of a moderately hot oven (Gas Mark 4, 350°F.) for about 1¼ hours.

Irish Boozy Cake

Not cheap, but a delicious large keeping cake that yields plenty of slices.

    ½ *lb. butter*
    3 *cups soft brown sugar*
    2 *lb. currants*
    8 *tbsp. sultanas*
    8 *tbsp. stoned or seedless raisins*
    4 *tbsp. mixed chopped peel*
    1½ *cups chopped blanched almonds*
    4 *cups plain flour*
    5 *large eggs*
    1 *level tsp. bicarbonate of soda*
    ½ *pint brown ale (or stout)*

Grease and line a 10 inch round cake tin with greased greaseproof paper. Cream together the butter and sugar till light and fluffy. Add the fruits, almonds and then the sifted flour and well beaten eggs. Warm the stout or brown ale slightly, add bicarbonate of soda, and when dissolved stir this liquid into the cake mixture. Mix well for 3 minutes. Transfer to prepared tin. Bake in centre of a cool oven (Gas Mark 2, 300°F.) for 2 hours, then reduce heat to very cool (Gas Mark $\frac{1}{2}$, 250°F.) for $1\frac{1}{2}$–$2\frac{1}{4}$ hours or till cooked through. Cool in the tin. Store in airtight tin or wrapped in kitchen foil.

Cherry Almond Cake

Keep 2 weeks before eating.

> $\frac{1}{2}$ *lb. margarine*
> 8 *level tbsp. granulated or caster sugar*
> $1\frac{2}{3}$ *cups plain flour*
> $\frac{1}{2}$ *tsp. baking powder*
> *pinch salt*
> 3 *large eggs*
> $\frac{3}{4}$ *cup ground almonds*
> *couple of drops almond essence*

Cream margarine and sugar till pale and fluffy. Stir in sieved flour, baking powder and salt alternately with beaten eggs. Add ground almonds and essence. Bake in 8 inch cake tin for 3 hours in very slow oven (Gas Mark $\frac{1}{2}$, 250°F.).

Honey-Raisin Ring Cake

> 1 *cup seeded raisins*
> 1 *cup soft butter or shortening*
> 1 *cup liquid honey*
> 4 *eggs*
> 1 *tsp. vanilla essence*
> 1 *tsp. lemon extract*
> 3 *cups sifted plain flour*

3 *tsp. baking powder*
1 *tsp. salt*
$\frac{1}{2}$ *cup chopped walnuts*

Grease and flour a ring tin. Chop raisins coarsely, cream butter or shortening until fluffy. Add honey and beat to blend well. Add eggs, one at a time, beating well after each addition. Stir in vanilla and lemon extract. Sift flour, baking powder and salt together into mixture and beat thoroughly. Stir in nuts and raisins. Spoon into the prepared ring tin, and bake at Gas Mark 2, 300°F. for about $1\frac{1}{4}$ hours or until a toothpick stuck into the cake comes out clean. Turn out of tin and cool on cake rack. Wrap in heavy foil and leave to mellow a few days before cutting.

Easy Dundee Cake

$\frac{1}{2}$ *cup glacé cherries, chopped*
$\frac{1}{2}$ *pint water*
10 *oz. margarine*
$1\frac{1}{2}$ *packed cups currants*
$1\frac{1}{2}$ *packed cups sultanas*
4 *tbsp. chopped mixed peel*
1 *large can condensed milk*
$2\frac{1}{2}$ *cups plain flour*
$\frac{3}{4}$ *level tsp. bicarbonate of soda*
pinch of salt
1 *oz. blanched almonds, split*

Line and grease an 8 inch cake tin. Place cherries, water, margarine, prepared fruit and condensed milk in a saucepan. Bring to the boil, simmer gently for 3 minutes and leave to cool. Add sieved flour, bicarbonate of soda and salt to the fruit mixture, beat well and pour into the prepared tin. Place almonds on top. Bake in a very moderate oven (Gas Mark 3, 325°F.) for 3 hours. Cool for 5 minutes before turning out.

(For a smaller cake, use *half* above ingredients and bake in a 6 inch cake tin for 2 hours.)

Golden Syrup Sponge

The syrup keeps it moist for about a week.

2 eggs
$\frac{3}{4}$ cup sugar
$\frac{3}{4}$ cup S.R. flour
2 tbsp. cornflour or custard powder
$\frac{1}{4}$ tsp. salt
1 tbsp. golden syrup
1 tbsp. butter
3 tbsp. water

Grease two $7\frac{1}{2}$-inch sandwich tins or an oblong 7 inch × 11 inch one. Beat eggs well for about half a minute, then add sugar. Beat a couple more minutes. Sift together flour, cornflour or custard powder and salt. Melt golden syrup with butter and water. Go on beating eggs and sugar till light coloured and frothy (when sugar will have melted). Gradually, stir melted mixture and dry ingredients, alternately, into the egg mixture. Mix well without beating, and with as little stirring as possible. Add a drop or two of vanilla if you like. Pour into tins and bake 20–25 minutes in a fairly hot oven (Gas Mark 6, 400°F.). When cool, store in an airtight tin and when ready to eat it sandwich together with some kind of butter icing, and sprinkle top with icing sugar (or use whipped cream to sandwich and/or top the cake).

One-Two-Three Cake

8 eggs, beaten
4 cups S.R. flour, sifted
$2\frac{3}{4}$ cups caster sugar
1 lb. margarine or butter

Cream butter and sugar, add eggs, beating well, then fold in the sifted flour. Divide mixture into three basins. Into one mixture blend coffee essence plus chopped walnuts to taste: into another stir 2 heaped tbsp. coconut; and into the third, stir 2 flat tbsp. drinking chocolate powder. As each mixture is well blended, tip it into a greased floured tin. The coconut into a flat oblong tin, the coffee and walnut into a loaf tin and the chocolate into an 8 inch round cake tin. Cook all three in a fairly hot oven (Gas Mark 6, 385°F.), the larger cakes near the top of the oven, the coconut bake below that. Timings, depending on position, are about 40 minutes for the coconut, and 1–1¼ hours for the coffee and walnut cake and the chocolate cake. Cover tops with greaseproof paper or foil if they reach the right, nice colour before being completely cooked.

Paulette's Cheese Cake

Ask for the cheapest quality cream cheese to make this.

> *pastry (using 2 cups sweet Pastry Mix on p. 39)*
> *1 lb. cream cheese*
> *juice of 2 lemons*
> *zest of 4 lemons*
> *sugar to taste (about 2 level tbsp.)*
> *sultanas to taste*
> *2 eggs, beaten*

Use the made-up pastry to line a greased, oblong tin. Put the cream cheese into a bowl, and beat till it's nice and creamy. Mix in everything else, put into pastry case. Bake in the middle of a moderate oven (Gas Mark 5, 375°F.) for 20–30 minutes. It will still seem soft, specially in the middle, but firms up as it cools.

Fudge Cake

The only cooking needed for this one is some saucepan heating.

> *2–3 oz. walnuts*
> *1 cup mixed fruits (sultanas, dates, peel etc.)*
> *1 egg*
> *½ cup brown sugar*
> *4 oz. butter*
> *1 tsp. vanilla*
> *½ lb. plain or sweet digestive biscuits*

Chop walnuts and mixed fruits. Into a pan break the egg, and add brown sugar. Beat together, then add butter. Cook gently till butter melts. Remove from heat, add vanilla. Crush biscuits, and tip into a basin. Tip melted mixture onto crumbs, add fruit and nuts, and stir till mixture is damp and crumbly. Tip into square shallow tin (if you want, line it with double thickness greaseproof paper, and have this hanging a couple of inches over each end of the tin so you can lift it out easily). Put in fridge or coldest place till firm. Lift out, then cut into squares or oblongs. (Variation is to add a rounded tbsp. cocoa to eggs and sugar.)

Aunty Olive's Shortbread

4 heaped tbsp. flour
8 oz. butter
4 level tbsp. caster sugar
8 level tbsp. desiccated coconut
6 level tbsp. ground rice

Blend butter into flour with fingertips, till the mixture is like fine breadcrumbs. Stir in sugar, coconut and ground rice. Put in greased shallow, square tin. Bake for about ¾ hour at Gas Mark 3, 325°F.

Shortbread Biscuits

4 level tbsp. sugar (granulated or caster)
8 oz. butter
1½ cups plain and 1½ cups S.R. flour
pinch salt

Melt butter, without boiling, stir in the dry ingredients. Beat well together, then divide the mixture into four, and flatten each piece into rings, about ½ inch thick, on a greased baking sheet. Cut each ring into eight fan shapes, separate slightly, and prick with fork. Bake for ¾ hour at Gas Mark 3, 325°F.

Date Fingers

> ½ lb. quick porridge oats
> 5 heaped tbsp. soft brown sugar
> 4 oz. chopped stoned dates
> 5 oz. butter

Mix together the oats, brown sugar and dates. Melt butter in a saucepan and then stir it into the oat mixture. Blend well and spread out in a shallow, oblong tin that's well greased. Bake in a moderate oven (Gas Mark 4, 350°F.) for 25–30 minutes. When cooked but still soft and warm, cut mixture into fingers. Don't try to remove from tin till quite cold.

Chocolate Coconut Biscuits

> ½ lb. margarine
> 8 level tbsp. sugar
> 6 heaped tbsp. S.R. flour
> 2 cups desiccated coconut
> 1 tbsp. cocoa

Soften margarine, cream with sugar. Work in other ingredients. Place mixture (very stiff) in oblong greased tin and press down. Bake 25 minutes in moderate oven (Gas Mark 4, 350°F.). Leave in tin to cool. Cut when cold. Cover with a chocolate or fudge icing (see pp. 237 or 238).

Tray Bake

> 4 oz. margarine
> 1½ packed cups sultanas
> 4 tbsp. cocoa
> 1 lb. semi-sweet biscuits, crushed
> 8 tbsp. sugar
> 2 eggs

Boil together margarine, sultanas, sugar and cocoa for 1 or 2 minutes. Add crumbs and beaten egg. Press into flat tin and leave to set. Cover with fudge icing (p. 237) if you like.

Refrigerator Cookies

Make up this biscuit dough when you have time, then store in the refrigerator ready to make instantly into hot, fresh cookies. Makes 60 small biscuits, or thereabouts.

> 4 oz. best quality margarine
> 12 tbsp. caster sugar
> 1 standard egg
> 1 tsp. vanilla essence
> 2 cups plain flour
> nuts or glacé cherries to decorate

Place all ingredients except nuts or cherries in a bowl, and mix together to form a soft dough. Knead lightly. Form into 2 (8 inch) long rolls and wrap each lightly in greaseproof paper.

Store in refrigerator for up to 2 weeks.

To cook: Prepare a moderate oven (Gas Mark 4, 350°F.). Lightly grease baking sheets. Cut cookie rolls in $\frac{1}{4}$ inch slices. Place a piece of nut or half a cherry on each slice, and place on baking sheets a little apart to allow for spreading. Bake in centre of oven for 15 to 20 minutes until pale golden brown. Remove from baking sheets and cool on a wire rack.

Meringues

If well dried in baking, then stored in an airtight container, meringues keep for weeks and make useful bases for puddings. Small ones can be a topping for fruit purées with ice cream and chocolate sauce. Large meringue cases can be baked, stored and filled when wanted with fruit and cream.

> 2 egg whites

*½ cup caster sugar (granulated will do if you've no caster, but
  you get a rougher, chunkier texture)*
vanilla essence or other flavouring

Beat egg whites till mixture stands up in peaks. Add half the sugar
to eggs and beat again till mixture is very thick. Gradually add rest
of sugar and flavouring, mixing long enough to blend, but no longer.
Place spoonfuls on oiled baking sheets, or on greased foil on a baking
sheet near bottom of a very slow oven (Gas Mark ¼, 250°F.). Bake
till completely dried and crisp, about 1–1½ hours. To test, lift one
out and press bottom with thumb – it should be firm. If squashy,
give the meringues a bit longer, to complete drying out. This makes
12 medium or 16 smaller meringues. Or cut two pieces of foil
(about 6 inch diameter) and spread mixture over these, to make 2
large round meringues.

If you want to make flavoured meringues add any of the following
to the mixture:

Coffee – 1–1½ tsp. soluble coffee.

Lemon – finely grated rind of 1 lemon.

Cornflake – 2 cups.

Chopped nuts and glacé cherries – to taste.

Almond – just before baking, sprinkle meringue tops with flaked
almonds.

N.B. If you use this meringue as a topping (i.e. for rice pudding)
use the basic mix, with sugar according to taste. Bake till lightly
coloured (about 30 minutes) at Gas Mark 3, 325°F. It's not meant to
be dried and crisp.

Chocolate Crunchies

6 oz. bitter chocolate
1 cup sweetened condensed milk
3½ cups cornflakes

Melt chocolate in basin over pan of hot water, or in pan over very low heat. Add condensed milk to it, and heat gently for 5 minutes or till mixture thickens. Cool. Stir in cornflakes. Place in spoonfuls in paper cases and bake at Gas Mark 5, 375°F., for 10–12 minutes. Remove onto rack to cool. Store in airtight container.

Bitty Bars

For about 36 small bars.

> 4 oz. semi-sweet biscuits
> 1 cup walnuts, chopped
> 4 oz. butter
> 1 (6 oz.) packet chocolate chips
> 12 tbsp. desiccated coconut
> 1 large can condensed milk

Prepare a moderate oven (Gas Mark 4, 350°F.). Place biscuits between 2 sheets of greaseproof paper and crush with a rolling pin. Chop walnuts. Place butter in a small saucepan, melt over a low heat, then pour into a shallow oblong baking tin. Then, sprinkle over it the following, in order given: crushed biscuits, walnuts, chocolate chips, coconut. Open can of condensed milk and pour this evenly over everything else. Bake in centre of moderate oven for 25 to 30 minutes, until lightly browned. Remove from oven and leave to cool for 15 minutes. Cut into slim bars, and remove from tin when cold.

Peanut Cookies

> 4 oz. butter
> 8 tbsp. caster sugar
> 1 egg
> 5 heaped tbsp. plain flour
> 1 level tsp. baking powder
> ½ tsp. salt
> 1 rounded tbsp. cocoa
> 8 oz. shelled, skinned peanuts

Cream the butter and sugar, then beat in the egg. Sift the flour, baking powder, salt and cocoa, and stir into the creamed mixture. Roughly chop the skinned peanuts, and add to the mixture. Put teaspoons of the mixture onto greased baking trays (30–35 of them). Bake in a moderately hot oven (Gas Mark 5, 375°F.) for about 15 minutes. Cool on a wire tray. Store in an airtight tin.

Macaroons

6 tbsp. caster sugar
¾ cup ground almonds
1 egg white
1 tbsp. ground rice
rice paper
blanched almonds

Whisk egg white till stiff, add dry ingredients, and drop in small heaps on rice paper on dry baking sheet. Brush each heap lightly with water to give smooth exterior. Top each macaroon with ½ blanched almond, and cook 20–30 minutes in slow oven (Gas Mark 1, 275°F.).

Family Loaf Cake

A good-size cake. And it stays fresh quite a while.

3 oz. warmed margarine
5 rounded tbsp. Bake Mix (p. 41)
4 tbsp. caster sugar
1 egg
¼ pint plus 1 tbsp. golden syrup, warmed
½ lb. ground almonds
1 lb. plain flour
¼ pint plus 1 tbsp. warm milk
¼ tsp. bicarbonate of soda

Put the fat into the mixing bowl and on top of it put the measured Bake Mix. Beat in the sugar, egg, syrup, ground almonds and all the milk, except 1 tbsp. Fold the flour into the well beaten mixture.

Dissolve the bicarbonate in the remaining warm milk and stir that into the mixture. Put into an 8 inch greased and floured cake tin, and bake for 1½–1¾ hours in a moderately hot oven (Gas Mark 4, 350°F.).

QUICK BREADS

Most families know what it's like to run out of bread unexpectedly. Making your own provides a solution, and here are recipes for some plain and not so plain breads, that need no yeast.

Emergency Rolls

Eat these *warm*. They don't keep well.

> 8 *heaped tbsp. flour*
> 4 *level tsp. baking powder*
> ½ *oz. butter*
> ½ *level tsp. salt*
> ½ *pint milk, or milk and water*

Sift together flour, baking powder and salt. Rub in fat. Add liquid and mix to soft dough. Turn onto a floured board and cut into eight pieces. Shape each piece into a roll. Place on well greased baking sheet, brush with milk and cook for 15 minutes near the top of a hot oven (Gas Mark 9, 500°F.).

Slow Walking Bread

> 4 *cups S.R. flour*
> 1½ *lb. mixed fruit*
> 1½ *cups soft brown sugar*
> ¾ *pint cold strained tea*
> 1 *egg*

Mix fruit and sugar and soak overnight in cold tea. Next day, add flour and beaten egg. Mix well. Put in a greased 2 lb. loaf tin.

Bake 1½–2 hours at Gas Mark 4, 350°F. Cover top with foil once it's brown enough. Turn onto wire rack. Serve sliced and buttered.

Scofa Bread

> 1½ *lb. scofa meal (sold in Health Food Shops)*
> 1 *tsp. salt*
> ¾ *pint milk or water*

Heat oven to Gas Mark 7, 425°F. Mix ingredients together well, and turn the dough onto a slightly floured surface. Mould into a dome-shaped round, then cut this into four triangular portions. Bake for 25–35 minutes till the crust browns, and a knife thrust in doesn't come out sticky. For variation, add some sultanas. Or work in a little butter or margarine.

Oaten Bread

Coarse textured, and nice eaten very fresh. Needs to be started 7 or 8 hours before you bake it, though.

> 1½ *cups porridge oats*
> 1 *pint sour milk (you can sour milk with a squeeze of lemon juice)*
> 4 *cups, minus 4 tbsp. of wholemeal flour*
> 1 *level tsp. salt*
> 2 *level tsp. bicarbonate of soda*

Soak the porridge oats in sour milk or buttermilk overnight or during the day for 7 or 8 hours. Next day sift the flour, salt and bicarbonate of soda, and mix into the soaked oats to make a firm dough. Knead lightly till smooth. Cut into four, and form each piece into a round about 2½ inch thick. Place on a floured baking tray, bake on second shelf from top in hot oven (Gas Mark 6, 400°F.) for 25–30 minutes till the rounds are brown and cooked through. Cool on a wire tray.

Brown Soda Bread (griddle)

To cook on a griddle or electric hotplate, or in a large-based, very heavy frying pan.

> 6 oz. *plain flour*
> 1 *level tsp. salt*
> 1½ *level tsp. bicarbonate of soda*
> 3 *level tsp. cream of tartar*
> ½ *tbsp. sugar*
> 6 *heaped tbsp. wholemeal flour*
> *a little less than* ½ *pint milk, or milk and water mixed*

Sift plain flour, salt, bicarbonate of soda, cream of tartar, and sugar into bowl. Add wholemeal flour, mix to soft dough with the milk, or milk and water mixed, using a knife. Turn onto floured board and shape into a flat round, about 1 inch thick. Heat a griddle, heavy frying pan or electric hotplate and grease lightly. Place the dough on the heated griddle and cut into four quarters. Lower the heat as much as possible, and cook for about 10 minutes till brown on the under side. Turn each piece and continue cooking gently till golden brown and cooked through (about 30–40 minutes in all).

This mixture will also make a 1 lb. loaf if baked in the oven.

Speedy Celery Bread

> 1 *egg*
> ½ *pint water*
> 1 *packet of celery soup* (1 *pint size*)
> 4 *cups S.R. flour*
> *level tsp. salt*
> 3 oz. *butter or margarine*
> *little milk for glazing*

Mix egg and water together. Blend in the dry soup mix and allow to stand for 10 minutes. Sieve flour and salt, and rub in butter or margarine. Pour in soup mixture and work ingredients together. Knead into a round. Lift onto a greased baking sheet, flatten slightly and brush with milk. Mark off eight sections diagonally and bake in a fairly hot oven (Gas Mark 6, 380°F.) for 35–40 minutes. Serve this celery bread freshly baked and well buttered, with salads, cheese or soup.

Walnut Bread

A sweet, tea-time loaf, this one.

> 1 *large egg*
> 1½ *cups granulated sugar*
> *pinch of salt*
> ½ *pint milk*
> 3 *cups plus* 1 *heaped tbsp. S.R. flour*
> 6 *oz. walnuts, grated*

Grease and line a 2 lb. loaf tin with greased greaseproof paper. Beat the egg and add the sugar, salt and milk. Mix in the sifted flour, and lastly the grated walnuts. Blend well and allow the mixture to stand for 15 minutes before cooking. Bake in the centre of a moderate oven (Gas Mark 4, 350°F.) for 1½ hours, or until cooked through. Turn out of the tin, remove the greaseproof paper and allow to cool. Serve sliced and spread with butter.

Malted Loaf

> 2 *cups Multi-Purpose Mix* (*p.* 42) *plus* 4 *extra tbsp. S.R. flour*
> (*or* 2 *oz. margarine and* 2 *cups plus* 2 *heaped tbsp. S.R. flour*
> *rubbed together*)
> 4 *tbsp. soft brown sugar*
> 2 *rounded tbsp. Ovaltine*
> ½ *cup sultanas*
> 1 *egg*
> 1 *tbsp. golden syrup*
> *enough milk for sticky consistency* (*about* ⅓ *cup*)

Beat everything well together, then put into a 2 lb. well greased and floured loaf tin. Bake for about 1 hour or till cooked through in the centre of a Gas Mark 3, 325°F. oven.

NO-COOK GOODIES

Everything in this section is *very* rich, so dole out with discretion.

No-bake Christmas Cake

> ¼ *lb. chopped dates*
> 1 *cup ground almonds*
> 1 *cup prunes, soaked overnight*
> 3 *pieces chopped preserved ginger*
> 6 *tbsp. raisins (seedless)*
> 2 *heaped tbsp. candied peel*
> 1 *tbsp. walnut halves*
> 1 *tbsp. glacé cherries*
> *vanilla icing for topping*
> *rice paper*

Mince all the fruits except the cherries and mix together, with the chopped ginger, peel and ground almonds. Line the bottom of an 8 inch cake tin with rice paper. Put in the mixture, and press well down. Cover with another layer of rice paper. Leave overnight in a cool place, then ice the top. Decorate with walnuts and cherries.

Rich Chocolate Slab

> *Biscuit crust (made as on p. 232)*
> 8 *oz. plain chocolate*
> 4 *tbsp. caster sugar*
> 2 *oz. butter or margarine*
> 3 *tbsp. top of the milk*

Grease a shallow 7 inch square baking tin, and line with greaseproof paper overhanging the sides. Sprinkle a layer of the biscuit crust over the base.

Break the chocolate into squares, and melt in a bowl over hot water. Add the sugar, butter and top of the milk. Beat till smooth, and leave over low heat for a couple more minutes. Then pour one-third of the chocolate mixture over the sprinkling of biscuit crust in the tin. Continue with layers, ending with the crust. Fold the paper over the cake, and keep cool till needed, preferably in a refrigerator. When it's time to serve the cake, remove from the tin by lifting it out on the greaseproof paper, to prevent it breaking up.

Mocha Treat

> $\frac{1}{2}$ lb. plain chocolate
> $\frac{1}{2}$ lb. butter or margarine
> 2 beaten eggs
> 1 tbsp. granulated sugar
> 2 oz. chopped walnuts
> coffee essence, to taste
> $\frac{1}{2}$ lb. broken sweet (but not cream) biscuits

Melt together the chocolate and the butter or margarine. Blend in the beaten eggs, sugar, chopped walnuts and coffee essence. Crush the broken sweet biscuits and gently stir these into the chocolate mixture. Put into an 8 inch sandwich tin that's lined with greased greaseproof paper. Chill 4 hours, or till firm and set. Keep any left-overs in the refrigerator.

Butter Refrigerator Cake

> 8 oz. biscuit crumbs (4 oz. sweet, and 4 oz. digestive)
> $3\frac{1}{2}$ oz. butter
> 2 level tbsp. caster sugar
> 6 level tbsp. cocoa (chocolate for a less strong flavour)
> 1 rounded tbsp. golden syrup

Roll biscuits into fine crumbs. Cream together butter and sugar

Add cocoa and syrup, and slowly add biscuit crumbs, mixing well. Put into a 7 inch well-greased sponge tin. Smooth top with a knife, and chill for 2–3 hours. Remove from ring, and ice with butter icing or fudge or glacé icing (see pp. 237–239).

Choco-Raisin Fingers

A useful way with forgotten, dried-up sponge.

> 8 *tbsp. stoned raisins*
> 4–5 *oz. sponge cake*
> 3 *oz. butter*
> 4 *oz. bar of plain chocolate*
> *grated rind of orange*
> 1 *tbsp. golden syrup*

Line a square tin with greaseproof paper overhanging the sides. Plump the raisins by leaving them in boiling water for a few minutes. Then drain and dry them. Roughly crumb the sponge, then melt the butter with the plain chocolate, and add to the crumb mixture, along with orange rind and golden syrup. Add the raisins. Press into tin to a depth of about ½ inch. When set, cut into fingers. Lift out on the greaseproof paper.

PASTRY PLUS ALTERNATIVES

There's no great mystique to pastry-making. It's all a matter of getting the proportions right, and of making the pastry as quickly as possible, because this way you handle it less and it stays cooler.

I'm forgetting about the more time-consuming traditional methods of making flaky or puff pastry. But the following pages give some guides to different types of pastry, plus a selection of casings that can act as substitutes if you really don't have pastry fingers.

Shortcrust Pastry

Go by weight for this, and use half the amount of fat that you do of flour. Then allow 2 level tsp. salt and approximately ¼ pint water to each pound of flour.

Sift the flour with the salt into a bowl, cut the fat (which can be lard, margarine, butter or a blend of any of these) into pieces, and rub the two together until completely blended. Then gradually work in the water (you may not need it all) until you have a soft but not sticky ball. Put onto a well floured surface, and roll and cut as needed.

As variations on the shortcrust theme, you can make:

Cheese Pastry: substitute egg yolks for liquid (using 2 egg yolks to each pound of flour, plus a little cold water if necessary) and add 8 heaped tbsp. finely grated, strong-flavour cheese.

Oatmeal pastry: Substitute 2 heaped tbsp. fine oatmeal for 2 heaped tbsp. of the flour.

Flan pastry: Add 2 level tbsp. caster sugar, and mix with 1 egg yolk and a little cold water instead of all water.

Quick-Mix Short Pastry

> 1½ *cups flour*
> ½ *tsp. salt*
> 4 *oz. fat (a mixture of half cooking fat and half butter or margarine). It's important that all the fat is soft.*

Add the fat to the flour along with 2–3 tbsp. cold water, and stir with a fork till well blended (if you're doing it in an electric mixer, use a moderate speed). Don't add more water unless it seems vital. Roll out and use as you need it.

Suet Pastry

See p. 40.

Corn Oil Pastry

2 cups flour
½ tsp. salt
8 tbsp. corn oil
cold milk

Sift the flour and salt together. Blend in the corn oil. Then stir in enough milk to make a smooth dough. Roll out gently between two sheets of waxed paper, and use like ordinary short pastry.

Cream Cheese Pastry

5 oz. butter or margarine
5 oz. carton cream cheese
2¼ cups plain flour

Cream the fat till soft, then blend in the cream cheese. Stir in the flour till the mixture binds together. Knead till smooth and free from cracks. Leave in the refrigerator for an hour, then roll out and use to line a 10 inch flan ring or pie dish. (Adjust quantities for a smaller or larger tin.) Line with aluminium foil so that the pastry doesn't rise in the centre. Bake on a shelf just above the centre of a hot oven (Gas Mark 6, 400°F.) for 20 minutes. Remove foil, then return to oven for 5 minutes, till crisped on the base surface.

Flan Pastry Using Bake Mix

To line a 10 inch flan tin, allow 4 heaped tbsp. Bake Mix (p. 41) to 8 rounded tbsp. of S.R. flour. Fold the flour into the mix, knead into a light dough, and mould it with floured hands to cover the well-greased, floured tin. Place a foil circle to cover the centre. Bake in a Gas Mark 5, 375°F. oven, for about 25 minutes, cool on a wire tray, and fill just before serving.

Speedy Flaky Pastry

Most kids love flaky pastry. But the turmoil of making it if you haven't got the knack and the house is awash with noise and activity, is generally just too much. Not done this way, though.

$\frac{1}{2}$ *lb. butter*
$\frac{1}{2}$ *lb. margarine or shortening*
3 *cups plain or S.R. flour*
$\frac{3}{4}$ *cup cold water*

Bring water to the boil in a pan. Meanwhile, roughly chop fats into small pieces. When the water starts to boil, pour it over the fats and stir till they're dissolved. Then stir in the flour vigorously till everything's completely blended. At this stage it will look liquid and a little curdled but don't *worry*. Put the mixture, still in its bowl, in the refrigerator or other cold place, and leave for several hours (overnight is best of all). By this time it will be firm and ready to roll out and use as you use ordinary flaky pastry. The whole of the actual making process takes about five minutes flat. And if you want to make it even more in advance, you'll be glad to know that it keeps in a cold place quite happily for a few days.

Quick Mix Biscuit Crust

$1\frac{1}{2}$ *cups S.R. flour*
pinch of salt
3 *oz. softened butter or margarine*
4 *tbsp. caster sugar*
1 *egg*

Sift flour and salt into a mixing bowl. Add the other things all at once to the bowl, and mix for about a minute or till well blended with an electric mixer (on slow speed) or hand mixer.

Roll out and use as needed for sweet flans, plate tarts, jam tarts, cheesecake and so on. Unless the filling demands otherwise, cook at Gas Mark 6, 400°F., for about 15 minutes.

Some Pastry Tips

Cooking times for pastry vary according to the type and the filling

As a general guide, unless the recipe says otherwise, a flan or other pastry case baked blind should generally go in a fairly hot oven (Gas Mark 6, 400°F.) and be cooked for about 20 or 25 minutes, or till the pastry is light brown.

A 'raw' pastry case containing a sweet or savoury filling takes about 30 minutes at the same oven setting. For a deep meat pie, follow the same procedure for the first half hour, and then reduce to Gas Mark $\frac{1}{2}$–1, 250–300°F., and continue cooking for *at least* another hour, depending on the meat. For a deep fruit pie, set the oven at Gas Mark 3–4, 350°F., and bake for about an hour, half-way down the oven (a shallow plate pie takes rather less).

Remember that bought puff pastry, rolled out and baked in squares, can be very useful. It can top hot or cold fruit pies. It can sandwich cream and strawberries; or cream plus a canned pie filling.

Children like pastry if it looks appetising. So, when making sweet pies, remember to brush the uncooked pastry lightly with beaten egg whites (stir leftover yolks into soups if you can't think what else to do with them, or whip them into a hot milk drink – both without boiling). Then sprinkle pastry surface with white or brown sugar before baking.

Using one of the pastry or alternative casing recipes in this chapter (but not suet crust which doesn't keep too well) get into the habit of making several pastry cases at one time, and keeping them in airtight tins. To make them, grease your baking tins lightly, line them with pastry, then bake the pastry cases blind, covering centre with a circle of foil (as mentioned already) or with a circle of greaseproof topped by a few dried beans. Another idea, if you want pastry cases that are nice and golden *outside*, is to turn your tin upside down, grease the outside, roll out the dough on a well floured surface, and then mould it round the greased exterior of the tin. Bake in a preheated oven (Gas Mark 6, 400°F.) for 15–20 minutes. When pale gold, remove tins from the oven, and put them, pastry side down, on a wire tray. Once they've cooled, the tins should slide easily out of the pastry cases, and you can finish cooking the insides by putting the cases, still on the wire tray, back into the oven for a few minutes.

Finally, if you normally have difficulty in rolling out pastry because it keeps breaking, try letting it rest in the refrigerator for an hour or so beforehand. This often helps.

Jiffy Casings (non-pastry)

Corn Flake Crumbs Crust

> 1 *cup corn flakes, crushed*
> 2 *tbsp. caster sugar*
> 2 *tbsp. finely chopped nuts*
> ⅓ *cup soft or melted butter*

Combine all together, and press to line a lightly greased tin. As a variation, omit the nuts, and use 4 tbsp. icing sugar instead of 2 of caster. Either way, there's no need for baking – just put into a refrigerator or cool place to firm up.

Mocha Crisp

> 4 *tbsp. golden syrup*
> 3 *tbsp. demerara sugar*
> 2 *oz. butter*
> 1 *tsp. vinegar*
> 5 *cups Rice Krispies*
> *few drops rum essence (optional)*

Well butter an 8 inch sponge tin. Heat the syrup and sugar, and when the sugar is dissolved, add the butter and vinegar and boil for 3 or 4 minutes, not too rapidly. Stir in the essence and cereal. Stir well. Press down into the tin. When set, turn onto a plate and use to hold blancmanges, whips, custards, etc.

Cheesy Crisps Crust

> 1 *heaped cup crushed crisps*
> 6 *level tbsp. strong-flavour grated cheese*

½ *level tsp. salt*
1½ *oz. softened butter*

Mix the crushed crisps and grated cheese together with the salt. Add the butter and mix thoroughly. Firmly pat the mixture over the bottom and sides of an 8 inch pie plate or sandwich tin. Bake for 10 minutes in a moderate oven (Gas Mark 5, 375°F.). Cool, and if possible chill. Pack with a cooked savoury filling – and *don't* re-heat the case before serving.

Chocolate Wholemeal Casing

6 *oz. digestive wholemeal or sweetmeal biscuits*
1 *oz. butter*
2 *oz. chocolate, grated*

Crush the biscuits into fine crumbs (the easiest way to do this is with a rolling pin, in a plastic bag). Heat the butter and chocolate in a basin standing in a pan of hot water till melted. Put the biscuit crumbs in a bowl, and mix in the chocolate and butter mixture using a fork. When blended, press to line the base and sides of a buttered 8 inch pie plate or sandwich tin. Leave to cool and harden, and don't re-heat before serving.

Biscuit Crust

1 *packet* (7–8 *oz.*) *digestive biscuits*
2 *oz. butter or margarine*
2 *level tbsp. caster sugar*

Crumble the biscuits in a bowl till fine, like sand. In a small pan, melt the butter. Pour onto the crumbs, then add the sugar and mix well. Press into a well-greased tin ready to take any sweet prepared filling.

Ginger Casing

10 *oz. crushed ginger snaps*
6 *oz. melted butter*

Blend well, then press into a buttered tin and leave to firm. Simple as that.

Breadcases

>   18 *thin slices crustless bread*
>   4 *oz. margarine, melted*

Roll over the bread slices with a rolling pin, to flatten them slightly. Cut into rounds, using a 3 inch plain cutter. Brush both sides of bread with margarine, and as you spread each slice, press into patty tins. Bake in a moderate oven (Gas Mark 4, 350°F.), on the second or third shelf from the top, for 20 to 30 minutes, till crisp and golden. Fill with whatever hot mixture you like, and serve hot.

Note: Depending how busy you are, you can either trim the bread to fit, after pressing into patty tins, or leave the ends sticking up and slice them off after.

Breadballs

Try these when you've no space for rolling out pastry.

>   2 *oz. fresh white breadcrumbs*
>   1½ *oz. butter*
>   8 *heaped tbsp. S.R. flour*
>   1 *tsp. salt*
>   *sprinkle of white pepper*
>   ½ *tsp. dried onion powder*
>   3 *tbsp. cooking oil*
>   1 *tbsp. milk*
>   *dried breadcrumbs*

Gently fry fresh breadcrumbs in the butter. When golden brown, remove, and put in a bowl already containing the flour, salt, pepper, onion powder, cooking oil and milk. Stir all together, adding a little more milk if necessary to make a soft dough. Drop tablespoons

236

of this dough into dry buttered crumbs from your store (see p. 49) or packet dried breadcrumbs, and roll into balls. Arrange these crisp coated balls on top of your favourite casserole about 45 to 50 minutes before the end of cooking, and bake uncovered at Gas Mark 5, 375°F.

FILLINGS AND TOPPINGS

Sugar Topping

4 tbsp. softened butter
⅔ cup brown sugar
2 tbsp. cream
chopped nuts or coconut

Bake any cake or tray bake for 5 minutes *less* than the recipe says. Remove from oven, but don't turn the oven heat off. Leave the cake or bake to cool, then spread it with the above ingredients, blended well together. Put the cake back for five minutes, or till the frosting bubbles.

Note: Remember the Streusel Topping, too, on p. 43.

Chocolate Fudge Icing

2 oz. plain cooking chocolate
1 tbsp. water
4 level tbsp. icing sugar
knob of butter

Warm all together over a low heat, till chocolate is melted and all is blended. Swirl over cake or biscuits' surface.

Fudge Icing

2 cups soft brown sugar
2 tbsp. butter
2 tbsp. top of milk

Boil slowly for about 2 or 3 minutes. Remove from heat, and beat well till beginning to 'turn' and thicken. Cover cake quickly.

Cream Cheese Icing

> 3 oz. *cream cheese*
> *juice of* 1 *lemon*
> *soft brown sugar, to taste*

Beat the cream cheese and lemon juice till the mixture is smooth. Beat in sugar till the icing is of spreading consistency, then use. This can make a good filling, as well.

Glacé Icing

To coat an 8 inch sandwich cake, or cover the top of a deeper 8 inch cake.

> 8 *level tbsp. icing sugar*
> 1 *tsp. lemon juice*
> 1 *tbsp. cold water*

Sieve icing sugar, add juice, and then gradually add the water, beating well to obtain a smooth consistency. The icing is ready when it can coat the back of a wooden spoon thickly. At this stage, use straight away for cakes or biscuits. Leave to set.

For different flavourings, omit the lemon juice and use coffee essence, a little concentrated chocolate liquid, or orange juice.

Chocolate Icing

> 1 *cup icing sugar*
> 2 *tsp. cocoa*
> *water as needed*

Sift icing sugar and cocoa, and then blend with water to the right smooth consistency.

Creamy Cocoa Icing

> 5 *tbsp. shortening*
> ½ *cup cocoa*
> 2⅔ *cups sifted caster sugar*
> 7 *tbsp. evaporated milk*
> 1 *tsp. vanilla*

Melt all the above together, until bubbling. Then beat till thick enough to spread without running.

Peppermint Chocolate Icing

Put chocolate covered peppermints onto the surface of the cake to be iced, and either pop it under a grill or put quickly into a hot oven for a minute or two. Then smear the melting peppermints over the cake surface with a wet knife or spatula for a tasty, two-tone icing!

Butter Cream

> 4 *oz. butter*
> 6–8 *level tbsp. caster or icing sugar*

Cream the two together till very smooth and fluffy. If you want it a little softer, beat in just enough cold milk for the right consistency.

Butter Icing

> 3 *oz. butter*
> 1⅓ *cups sieved icing sugar*
> *milk, water or fruit juice as liked*

Soften the butter, then beat in the icing sugar. Add enough liquid to give a good consistency. Flavour and colour to taste.

For mocha butter icing, use black coffee instead of the above liquids. For chocolate butter icing, proceed as above, but add 6 level tbsp. cocoa, pre-mixed with a little boiling water.

CHAPTER NINE

Drinks

COLD DRINKS

Lemon Squash

> 6 *lemons*
> 3 *pints water*
> 3 *lb. sugar*
> 2 *oz. citric acid*

Squeeze lemons. Roughly cut up peel and pith, and put with juice and pips in a large jug. Add citric acid, sugar and water. Leave about 12 hours, with occasional stir, till all sugar has dissolved. Strain and bottle, dilute as needed.

Prune and Lemon Nog

For six servings.

> 2¼ *cups chilled prune juice*
> 3 *tbsp. lemon juice*
> 3 *cups milk*
> 3 *well beaten eggs*
> *sugar to taste*

Blend chilled prune juice with lemon juice. In another bowl, gradually add milk to the well beaten eggs. While whisking this mixture together gradually add prune juice mix. Sweeten to taste.

Ice Cream Sodas

To each glass, allow a tbsp. fruit juice. Add a large spoonful of vanilla ice cream and fill with iced soda water. To ice the soda water, stand the syphon in a fridge or on ice for 2 or 3 hours.

Orange Punch

For six servings.

> 1½ *pints orange juice*
> ¾ *pint ginger ale*
> *slices of orange*

Combine orange juice and ginger ale, and serve thoroughly chilled, garnished with slices of orange.

Ginger 'Champagne'

For a crowd.

> 1 *cup sugar*
> 1 *cup water*
> ¼ *cup orange juice*
> 1 *cup grapefruit juice*
> 1 *quart ginger beer*
> *sliced orange*

Boil sugar and water, and add fruit juices. Chill. Chill ginger beer separately. Mix just before serving and garnish with slices of orange.

Tomato Milk Drink

Per serving.

> 2 *tomatoes (skinned)*
> ¼ *cup water*
> 2 *tbsp. instant milk powder*
> ½ *tsp. celery salt*

If you have a liquidiser dump everything into it and whizz it around a few moments till blended. Otherwise, mash up tomatoes. Blend water with milk powder and then beat everything together.

Tomato Cheese Drink

Per serving.

> ½ cup chilled tomato juice
> 2 oz. cottage cheese
> pinch celery salt
> more salt to taste

Whip everything up together, by hand or in liquidiser.

Banana and Pineapple

Per serving.

> 1 large peeled ripe banana
> 2 tbsp. instant milk powder
> ½ cup canned pineapple juice

Mash the banana, blend the milk powder with the pineapple juice and then whip together. Or blend everything together in liquidiser.

Syrup Shake

For six servings.

> 2 pints cold milk
> 6 tbsp. golden syrup
> pinch salt

Shake or whisk mixture till well blended and frothy. Serve immediately in chilled glasses.

Soothing Syrup

For coughs and colds, try this one. Just heat 1 tbsp. blackcurrant jam in a tumbler of boiling water, then add a grating of nutmeg.

Chocolate Syrup

Blend 1½ tbsp. cocoa, 4 tbsp. sugar, dash salt and 1 cup water. Simmer gently for 5 minutes. Remove from heat and add 1 tsp. vanilla essence. Cool and store in covered jar in cool place. Use 2 tbsp. syrup to each cup of milk.

Caramel Syrup

Stir 1 lb. sugar into ½ pint water. Simmer gently 5 minutes. Cool. Add 1 tsp. vanilla essence and 2 tbsp. caramel syrup (made by caramelising 2 tbsp. brown sugar in 1 tbsp. water in heavy pan over steady heat). Bottle when cold and use 1 tbsp. to each glass of milk.

Orange and Lemon Drink

Per serving.

> 1 *large orange*
> 2 *tbsp. lemon juice*
> *water or soda water*
> *sugar if needed*

Cut orange in half and cut off one thin slice from its centre. Squeeze juice from remainder of orange. Place juice in a glass with lemon juice, and top up with water or soda water. Sweeten if wanted. Decorate glass with slice of orange.

Orange Nog

For six servings.

> *grated rind of 3 oranges*
> 1½ *pints milk*
> ½ *level tsp. cinnamon*
> 6 *standard eggs*
> *sugar to taste*

Place rind in saucepan with milk, cinnamon and sugar. Bring just to the boil then remove from heat. Whisk eggs together in basin and pour milk over them. Continue whisking until frothy. Pour into glasses and serve immediately.

Coffee Velvet

For six servings.

> 1 *family size block vanilla ice cream*
> 4 *tbsp. Camp coffee essence*
> 1½ *pints well chilled milk*

Cut up ice cream and place in bowl or jug. Add coffee essence and milk and whisk until smooth. Pour into glasses. Serve at once.

Apple Foam

For three–four servings.

> 1 *cup apple purée*
> *large can evaporated milk*
> 1 *cup cold water*
> *sugar to taste* (*caster*)

Blend all together either in liquidiser, or beating well. Chill. Just before serving, whisk up again.

Everlasting Ginger Beer

Ages ago I was given a 'ginger beer plant' and all through one long hot summer, by feeding the plant with sugar and ginger each day, we were able to have bottles and bottles of cheap ginger beer. Then the plant died. It wasn't till years later that I was given this recipe which is the 'starter' for home-made ginger beer – and continues to supply the 'plant' for successive brewings!

Begin by putting 1 rounded tsp. caster sugar in ⅓ pint warm water. Add ½ oz. active bakers' yeast, whisking in with fork. Leave in warm place for 10 to 15 minutes. Add ⅔ pint warm water and 1 rounded tsp. ginger. Put into a jar and cover loosely. Each day for 10 days, add 1 rounded tsp. ginger and 1 rounded tsp. caster or granulated sugar. Stir in and then leave to settle. On the 11th day, dissolve 12 oz. granulated sugar in 1 pint boiling water. Add 2 tbsp. lemon juice (or the juice of 1 large lemon), 2 pints cold water and the liquid from your jar (retaining the thick mush or 'plant' at the bottom). Bottle, cork, and keep for a few days, or up to three weeks before drinking. (Best kept in an outhouse or somewhere similar, and opened warily, since the occasional bottle has been known to explode!)

You can start the process all over again – but divide the plant in half (there's always someone glad of it, plus the recipe) unless you want to double up on all the ingredients.

HOT DRINKS

Chocolate Whip

Per serving.

> 2 *tbsp. chocolate syrup* (*p.* 243)
> 1 *egg*
> 1 *cup hot milk*

Whip together the chocolate syrup and egg till frothy. Whisk this into 1 cup hot milk. Dust with grated nutmeg.

Marshmallow Float

Drop one or two white or pink marshmallows onto hot drinks of chocolate, lemon or apple juice. Sip as it melts.

Coffee-Choc

Blend a half and half mixture of hot black coffee and hot chocolate, made with milk (some kids prefer evaporated milk in this). Sweeten to taste, and if you have any leftover thick cream around, float a blob on the top of each drink.

Hot Apple

At the bottom of each glass put 1 tbsp. apple purée. Pour on either hot water or hot milk, and sweeten to taste.

Hot Banana

For six servings.

>2 *pints milk*
>4 *bananas*
>2 *flat dstsp. caster sugar*

Blend the bananas with caster sugar, and put some of the resulting mixture at the bottom of each glass. Top up with hot milk, stir vigorously and serve piping hot.

Hot Savoury Drink

For six servings.

>4 *level tsp. meat extract*
>1 *pint boiling water*
>$\frac{3}{4}$ *pint hot tomato juice*
>*salt and pepper*

Place meat extract in a jug, add boiling water, and stir until dissolved. Add tomato juice and a little salt and pepper. Mix well and pour into glasses.

French Chocolate

Make drinking chocolate as usual, but first blend the chocolate with a little boiling water and a few drops almond essence. (Can be served chilled, too.)

Raspberry Noggin

For 2–3 servings.

Melt 8 marshmallows in a basin over hot water. Add 4 tbsp. raspberry jam. Pour in 1 pint hot milk and whisk well. Serve immediately.

Index

253

INDEX